Getting Your 'It' Together

Printed in the United States of America. No part of this book may be used or reproduced in any manner whatsoever without the express written permission of the author. For information, contact Hawkeye Richardson, 7925 N. Oracle Rd., PMB #176, Tucson, AZ, 85704.

Disclaimer

The information contained in this book is intended to be educational and not for diagnosis, prescription, or treatment of any physical, emotional or medical disorder whatsoever. This information should not replace consultation with a competent healthcare professional. The intent of the author is only to offer information of a general nature to help you in your quest for emotional and spiritual well-being. The author and publisher are in no way liable for any misuse of the material and assume no responsibility for your actions.

Copyright © 2009 Hawkeye Richardson
All rights reserved.
ISBN: 1-4392-2701-2
ISBN-13: 978-1439227015

Visit www.booksurge.com to order additional copies.

HAWKEYE
RICHARDSON

GETTING YOUR 'IT' TOGETHER
Simple Suggestions for
Attracting The Life You Want

2009

Getting Your 'It' Together

TABLE OF CONTENTS

Introduction   xi

PART 1: It's Okay to Have a Life

Chapter 1: Simple Suggestions for Attracting
   the Life You Want   1
Chapter 2: If Something Is Useful, Must You
   Understand How It Works?   5
Chapter 3: When Is Enough, Enough?   9
Chapter 4: The Role of the Subconscious Mind in
   Attracting the Life You Want   15
Chapter 5: Three Things that Keep You from
   Attracting the Life You Want   23
Chapter 6: Documenting What We Want   33
Chapter 7: Too Busy Being Busy   37
Chapter 8: Navigating the River of Life   43
Chapter 9: We All Come from Dysfunctional Families   47

Part 2: It's All About Feeling Good

Chapter 10: The Vibrations of Words   51
Chapter 11: You Only Feel Bad If You Think You Do   57
Chapter 12: Feeling Good by Not Feeling Bad   63
Chapter 13: Learning From Bad Feelings   71
Chapter 14: Feeling Good the Wrong Way   79
Chapter 15: Too Many Choices Can Make Us Unhappy   83
Chapter 16: There Is No Such Thing As a Bad Decision   89

Part 3: It's Okay to Be You

Chapter 17: Will the Real 'Me' Please Stand Up?	95
Chapter 18: Dr. Jekyll or Mr. Hyde?	103
Chapter 19: I Can't See the Forest for the…Me's?	109
Chapter 20: I Want to Be Like Mike	113
Chapter 21: I've Got the Pedal to the Metal, But My Parking Brake's On!	119
Chapter 22: Allowing the Good to Come Into Your Life	125
Chapter 23: You Are a Perfect Attractor	131
Chapter 24: Celebrating Our Successes	135
Chapter 25: Opportunity Just Knocked. Were You Listening?	139
Chapter 26: Big Boys Don't Cry	143

Part 4: Being Yourself in the World

Chapter 27: No News Is Good News	147
Chapter 28: Black Holes Suck	155
Chapter 29: Suffocated by an 800 lb. Gorilla	159
Chapter 30: Some Days I Feel Like I'm Fighting a Losing Battle	163
Chapter 31: Efficiency Experts	167
Chapter 32: Dead Batteries	175
Chapter 33: I'm Going 'Green'	181

Part 5: Living a Life with Others

Chapter 34: Having to Change Is a Royal Pain in the Butt!	185
Chapter 35: Misery Loves Company	195

Chapter 36: Are You For or Against?	201
Chapter 37: Conflict Resolution	205
Chapter 38: Grumpy Employees Attract Grumpy Customers	211
Chapter 39: The IDM File	215
Chapter 40: Making a List and Checking It Twice	221
Chapter 41: Helping Others Feel Good	225

Part 6: Putting 'It' All Together

Chapter 42: A Simple Plan for Living	229
Chapter 43: Getting Your 'It' Together	235

To Tess & Darcy

*The Best Reasons Why
I Want To Get My 'It' Together.*

INTRODUCTION

Once upon a time in a distant land, there lived a guru. He was known far and wide for his great wisdom. In the small town where he lived, he ran a school. Many students came, seeking the wisdom of the master.

One day, one of the students had a burning question that he wanted to ask the guru. Unfortunately, the master had gone into the mountains to rest and meditate and he would not return for a number of days. The determined student decided that the next day he, too, would climb into the mountains, find the master, and get his question answered.

Early the next morning, the student struck out on his journey. By midmorning, he reached the base of the mountain and started the long, steep climb to the top. After much effort, the student finally crested a ridge to find a beautiful clearing that overlooked the entire valley. And there, in the middle of the clearing, sat the master.

Not wanting to disturb his master, the student walked slowly into the clearing and sat down a few yards away. He decided that it would be best to sit quietly until the master acknowledged his presence, and then he would ask his question.

As the student sat, he noticed that the master was working on something with his hands. It appeared to be a lump of clay that he was molding and shaping into various forms.

The master continued to work and appeared oblivious to the student's presence. Knowing that he still had to climb back down the mountain and get home before dark, the student finally decided he could wait no longer, so he addressed the master.

Student:	"Oh great master, I'm sorry to bother you but I have an important question that I must ask you. May I interrupt your work long enough to seek your wisdom?"
Master:	"Why, of course my son. I would be happy to help in anyway I can. What is it you wish to know?"
Student:	"Well, I have a very important question that brought me here, but before I ask it, I wonder what it is that you are doing. It seems to be of great importance to you."
Master:	"Oh, this. Oh, it's not really all that important. I just come up here once in a while to get my 'it' together."

***

"…*I just come up here once in a while to get my 'it' together.*" Were you surprised to hear a guru make that statement? When most people picture a guru, they envision a person who already has his 'it' (his life) together.

But, why is that? Why is it that many of us believe we are the only person in the world who doesn't have his or her 'it' together? The truth is that we all have to work at getting our 'it' together, even gurus. More importantly, getting our 'it' together is not a one-time event. It is an on-going, lifetime process. To use an old analogy, it's a journey, not a destination.

Please understand that this is not a book about religion, secrets, meditation or affirmations. I understand and accept that those concepts bring comfort and peace to many people. If you are person who finds these things helpful in creating the life you want, then count your blessings and be happy in the good life you are living. Unfortunately, there are those among us who are still searching for something that seems to be missing in our lives.

Let me also assure you that this is not a book about me. While I use some of my own life experiences as examples, I offer them only as a means to stimulate thoughts about your own life.

I don't pretend to be a great philosopher or poet or teacher. I'm just a regular guy who keeps looking for ways to improve the quality of my life, and the lives of those I love. I don't claim to have *"The Answer"* or to know *"The Secret"* to creating a perfect life. I am not telling you *"The Way"*; I only wish to offer thoughts on how you can find *"Your Way"*.

I am not the first person who has offered ideas about attracting the life we want. There are many writings and oral traditions that deal with this concept. The *"I Ch'ing"* was composed in China almost five thousand years ago. The Bible, the Koran, the Torah and many other books contain the essence of attraction.

So, why did I decide to write this book when others have already offered their thoughts and guidance? I wrote it because the world continues to change. While the writings of the past provided great guidance to many people in their time, I find that I have trouble relating old teachings to the complex, technological world of today.

There is a quote by Thor Heyerdahl that expresses the difficulty I encounter while trying to live in the present world:

*"Progress is man's ability to
complicate simplicity."*

I have never come across a written or unwritten law that says life is supposed to be easy. However, I also have never found a law that says we are supposed to make life any harder or more complicated than necessary.

Personally, I find life to be more enjoyable when I keep things as simple as possible. When I say "as simple as possible", that does not mean that everything is simple and easy. It just means that life works better when I focus my intention on doing things in the simplest way I can.

In this book, I want to share some simple ideas that you can apply to the real-life situations you encounter in your daily life. I want to share information that will help you focus your thoughts and actions so you can reduce the amount of static in your life and be free to live a life more in alignment with your natural self.

I have tried to stay consistent with my own nature by writing in the simple style I enjoy: short words, short paragraphs, small chapters, and a belief that less is more. If you are looking for flowery prose, go read a novel.

Most chapters can be read in a few minutes. My intent is to convey ideas and suggestions in a few words that you can keep in mind during the day. I have also included some humor, as strange as it may be. I believe that laughter is the single best remedy for getting us out of our doldrums and back on the path to attracting the life we want.

My desire is to bring a smile to your face, perhaps a tear to your eye, and for you to become passionate about attracting the life you want. My hope is for you to come away with a clear understanding that you are the only person who can decide what you want in life. No one else can decide for you, and no one else can ever truly know what makes you feel good. Only you have the power to clear the static out of your vibrations so that you can live a life in harmony...with yourself.

1
Simple Suggestions for Attracting the Life You Want

The inspiration for this book came when a friend gave me two books: *"The Law of Attraction"* and *"Money and the Law of Attraction"* by Jerry and Esther (and Abraham) Hicks. My friend said, *"Just read them and keep an open mind to the concept. Then, let's talk about it after you have read them."*

After reading about the *"Law of Attraction"* in the Hicks' books, I found I liked the idea of focusing my attention on attracting the life I want. Since I consider myself to be a fairly sensible, feet-on-the-ground, left-brain-oriented type of guy, this reaction surprised me. Born in Missouri, I have always taken to heart the state motto: *"Show Me."*

(Note: The basic premise of Attraction is that 'like attracts like.' We attract those things that vibrate in the same way we do. However, we are always attracting, whether we do it consciously or unconsciously. Thus, we may attract things into our lives that we didn't desire because we have not clearly defined and focused on attracting what we want.)

Once I found myself interested in this idea of attraction, I had to ask myself the question: *"Why am I interested in a concept that doesn't seem to have much concrete, real-world proof behind it?"*

To be honest, I don't know if the *"Law of Attraction"* as presented in the Hick's books is real or true or omnipresent throughout the Universe. I don't know if I have a physical presence and then die and revert to some other kind of energy or state of existence. Frankly, I have no clue whether I'm more likely to come back as a powerful black hole, or an unconscious donut hole.

Regardless of this lack of clarity about my existence, I came to the realization that no amount of time spent thinking about the past or worrying about the future has ever gotten me closer to what I want. In my life experience, I find I am happiest when I stay focused on what I want, what I like, who I like being with, and places I like to be. When I focus on those things, I attract more of those things. For me, that is sufficient evidence to use the concept of attraction as a way to guide my life.

Before I offer my suggestions about using the idea of attraction as a simple guide for directing your thoughts and actions, however, I want to be clear about a couple of things.

Have I 'attracted' some unpleasant things into my life? Yes. Probably not as unpleasant as some people have experienced, but unpleasant enough that I don't wish to repeat them.

I'm pretty sure that I never consciously sent forth a desire to be kidnapped at gunpoint by two escaped convicts, along with my fiancé, two days before we were to be married. Fortunately, we lived to tell about it.

Unless you have been through such an event, you can't imagine how strange it is to be driving to the store to pick up your tuxedo, and hear your name being talked about on the news; or finding your picture on the front page of a major metropolitan newspaper as the big story of the day.

Why did I attract that event into my life? I don't know. Probably never will. Perhaps I just got too close to two escaped murderers running for their lives and I attracted them because my own vibrations were not clear enough to keep me out of harms way.

Whatever the case, let's be realistic here. Once that situation was over, I didn't pick up my *"List of Things I Want to Do in My Life before I Die"* and put a check mark next to 'be kidnapped'.

I can't promise you that anything you might learn from reading this book will prevent you from attracting the 'bad things that sometimes happen to good people.' The world is just too big and too complicated to be able to come up with a contingency plan for all possibilities.

What I do offer, however, is a clear belief that focusing on what you don't want, on what you don't have, and on what you think you may have done poorly in the past, will <u>not</u> get you closer to what you want in the future. I believe that we are more likely to get what we want in life when we focus our thoughts, our intentions, our energies, and our vibrations on what we want. For me, that plan seems to be as simple as I can make it.

The idea of taking personal responsibility for attracting what I want into my life feels good. I have tried living my life dwelling in the past, worrying about the future, and complaining about the now. Subconsciously, I believe I knew that living that way didn't make me happy; it never moved me closer to what I wanted from life. Therefore, as a logical, left-brain-oriented person, I came to what I considered to be a logical conclusion...the old way wasn't working. Thus, it was only logical to try a different way.

The concept of attraction puts the responsibility for my life squarely on me. That is exactly where the responsibility should be...in my own hands, mind and heart. It is my responsibility to focus my actions, my thoughts, and my intentions to create the life I want to attract.

The concept of attraction also meets one of my other main operating criteria...it is simple. As I mentioned in the *"Introduction"*, the more simply I do things, the better my life is. With the concept of attraction, all I have to remember is that I attract what I create with my thoughts, vibrations, actions, and beliefs. Simple.

In the following chapters, I will offer my thoughts on this concept of attraction. I will talk about how the concept works in our lives. I'll show you that you are already experiencing the effects of attraction, but in ways that you may have not noticed.

I will discuss how things we do subconsciously may prevent us from attracting what we desire, and how they may attract things we don't particularly want. I will also offer simple ideas to help you stay focused on what feels good.

***

The world in which we live places many demands and negative vibrations on us that are often difficult to ignore. Many aspects of our basic culture force unwanted static into our lives. Only by being conscious of what we want, and consistently focusing on what we want, are we able to get our it together and attract the life we seek.

2
If Something Is Useful,
Must You Understand How It Works?

Do you know how a magnet can attract a nail from a foot away? You can't see the attractive force. You can't smell it, taste it, or hear it. Even if you put your hand between the magnet and the nail, you can't feel anything going through your hand.

Can you see the gravity that keeps you on the ground? Can you feel the gravity that keeps the moon revolving around the earth? Can you hear the gravity that pulls your peanut butter sandwich facedown onto the floor when it falls off the kitchen counter?

No, you can't. But, if you can't see, hear, feel, taste or smell these things, why do you believe they exist? The reason most of us believe that gravity and magnetism are real is because we can see the effects they have on the world around us. We can't see the thing, but we can see the effect.

The concept of attraction is a similar thing. We can't see it or touch it or hear it. We can't smell it or taste it. The question is, can we see any effect that attraction has on the world around us? Yes, I think we can. Unfortunately, many of us (or maybe most of us) may not believe that the effects of attraction are real because we haven't taken the time to notice that we are, in fact, attracting much of what we get in life.

You may feel that it can't possibly be true that you have attracted everything that has happened in your life. Surely you didn't wish to get ill. You're pretty sure you didn't ask to be robbed at gunpoint. And you definitely know that you didn't ask to marry a spouse whose mother was the prototype for the Creature from the Black Lagoon.

So, if some of those negative things weren't on the list of what you wanted to attract, why did they come into your life? The truth is, I don't know. I don't know why we attract some unpleasant things.

That probably wasn't the answer you were hoping to hear, was it? I understand. That answer doesn't exactly have a good feeling to it, does it?

For the moment, let's look at this from a different perspective. Let's assume that it wasn't attraction that brought some of those less-than-pleasant things into your life. If it wasn't attraction, what did bring them to you? Are you just an unlucky person? Did you come into life with a chip on your shoulder? Did you step on a crack at an early age and end up breaking your mother's back?

Were you born under the wrong astrological sign? Did the doctor face you the wrong way when you made your entrance into the world and end up slapping you in the mouth? Did a crazed witch doctor put a curse on you and your family back in Neanderthal times?

Yes, I know. These are silly examples to use to try to explain why your life may not be quite what you had hoped for. But, I offer them to make a point. Even if one of these things was the cause, we still have a problem. We still can't see, taste, feel, hear, smell or positively identify that any of those potential causes are the reason why certain things happen in our lives. They are just as unknowable as the concept of attraction seems to be. Thus, we are left without a way to definitively explain why things happen in our lives.

The fact is, we may not ever know why things are the way they are in life. Nevertheless, we don't get to sit on the sidelines of life just because we don't understand the rules of the game.

Nowhere is it written that life will always be predictable, easy, or knowable. I'm sorry if that was what you were hoping to find here during your physical life. But, the truth is, it's a really big universe out there, and much as we might like to believe otherwise, we may never know why everything is the way it is.

This raises an interesting question. Could it be that it is the search for knowledge and understanding that makes life exciting and worth living? If we knew the answer to everything and if we knew exactly how our lives would go, what would be the point of living? Perhaps it is through the surprises in our lives that we learn the most about who we are and what we want.

Since we may not get to know why certain 'not-wanted' things happen in our lives, what are we going to do about it? While we may not know why we attract certain things into our lives, continuing to focus attention on the bad stuff is unlikely to attract what we do want.

Hence the question which is the title of this chapter. Do you have to understand why or how something works before you give it a try? If so, then the concept of attraction may not be of much use to you. If you already have some alternative idea that helps you stay focused on your wants, great. *"If your life ain't broke, don't fix it."* Use whatever concepts help you stay focused and make you feel good.

If, however, what you have been using hasn't worked as well as you had hoped, why not try a different approach? Why not use the idea of attraction to help you focus your thoughts, energy, actions and vibrations on what you want? It couldn't hurt any more than when the doctor slapped you.

***

To help you get started on your journey toward the new life you want to attract, I hereby use my power as Master of the Universe to decree that all previous curses put upon you and your tribe by crazed witch doctors are hereby removed forever. You are now free to move about the universe without fear of being attacked by vampire bats. (However, in the future, please try to refrain from making surly comments about the bone in the nose of the witch doctor's wife. She is very self-conscious about it and her husband does <u>not</u> take kindly to anyone who makes fun of her!)

3
When Is Enough, Enough?

In a five-day work week there are 120 total hours (5 x 24 = 120). Assuming a person gets seven hours of sleep per night, we use a total of 35 hours of our work week sleeping. This leaves 85 hours.

For the average person who works an 8:00 to 5:00 job, we spend 40 hours a week at our job. Add in an hour for lunch and an hour for commuting and we end up spending about 50 hours a week away from home earning a paycheck. Subtracting this from the available 85, we now have 35 hours left in our five-day week.

What is the purpose of this calculation? The purpose is to show that in our waking hours during the week, we spend 15 hours more time working than living our life. (50—35 = 15) Is it any wonder that our work has such a large impact on our lives?

"But, I have to work to earn a living," you say. That is true for most of us. The problem is, we have been brainwashed to believe that we have to earn tons of money to get the life we want. At the heart of the problem is the fact that most of us have not done a good job of defining, documenting and pursuing the life we want. If we had, I believe many of us would be much happier.

The difficulty we confront when we haven't defined what we want is that there is no way for us to know when enough is enough. The definition of the word "enough" is:

> *"Adequate for the want or need; sufficient for the purpose or to satisfy a desire."*

"Adequate for the want..." Please pay attention because this is *very* important. Enough is not defined as keeping up with the Joneses. Enough is not measured by comparing what you have to someone else. Enough is not defined as a bigger home, a faster car, or a bigger paycheck.

Enough means that something is sufficient to satisfy your want or desire.

Logic would lead us to understand that we cannot determine what is enough until we determine what we want. Once we have determined what we want, we can figure out how much is enough to satisfy those wants.

Unfortunately, most of us have gone about this whole process, shall we say, 'bass-ackwards.' In truth, most of society operates from the totally different paradigm of simply wanting 'more.'

More, more, more. I need to earn more. I need to have a bigger house. I need to send my kids to better schools. Unfortunately, there is one major problem with the concept of 'more':

<u>**More is never enough. More will never be enough.**</u>

Why? Because, by itself, 'more' has no defined want that can be satisfied. There is nothing to measure 'more' against to determine if a want has been satisfied. Therefore, <u>more can never be enough</u>.

If you think about people you know who are satisfied with their lives, satisfied with their work, satisfied with their place in the universe, what would you say is the source of their satisfaction? Are they always striving to have more? Or are they satisfied because they have enough? The people I know who seem to get the most satisfaction out of life appear to have a good grasp of what is 'enough' for them to be...dare we say...happy.

There is an old song about a farmer of simple means who is talking to a friend about what he has. In the song this farmer says:

"I've gotta humpback mule, a cow and a tater patch, eggs that are gonna hatch someday, I've got the Lord above and a good girl to love me, I'm the richest man, yessiree,...in all of the world."

In our more, more, more-oriented world, many people would hear this farmer and immediately think, *"Man, what world are you living in? Don't you want a new tractor and a big screen TV and a new car? Don't you care about what college your kids will go to? And this place of yours, just 20 measly acres. Man, you need at least a thousand acres before you can call it a real farm. I guess you just don't want to work hard enough to earn money for the finer things in life and to improve yourself."*

Our society has even gone to the trouble to develop stereotypes of people who seem to be content with what they have. Those stereotypes are almost always uncomplimentary. In fact, in most cases, we either denigrate or dismiss as slackers those people who are content having 'just enough.'

Ski bums. Beach bums. Artists. Musicians. When was the last time you heard a parent say they wanted their son or daughter to grow up and be a ski bum? The question is, are doctors happier than ski bums? Are lawyers more satisfied with their lives than musicians? Are any of us more content than that farmer who has "*...a mule, a cow, a girl who loves him, and eggs that are gonna hatch someday?*"

If I asked you how much money you would need to be able to say "*I have enough*," how much money would that be? Take your time. Give it some thought. A million dollars? Two million? Ten million? Are you having trouble coming up with a number that you know is 'enough?'

Do you know why it is so hard for you to come up with a number that you <u>know</u> would be enough? Because you haven't specifically identified the important wants in life that you are trying to satisfy. And, until you determine what those wants are, you will never be able to come up with a dollar figure that you know is enough.

What are you working for? If you started working two jobs and earned twice as much, would you satisfy your wants twice as fast? Will two cows make you more content than one cow if you don't have a guy or a girl who loves you? Is that 'nest egg' you keep putting money into going to satisfy your wants when it eventually gets around to hatching?

If you work at a job you hate just so you can 'have more,' what's the point? Until you define your wants, you will never be able to work long enough or hard enough to satisfy your needs.

What would it be like if you could work fewer hours, make less money, and actually satisfy more of your real wants? What would it be like to work at something you love knowing that the amount of money you earned would be 'more than enough'? What would it be like to wake up in the morning knowing you were going to go to work and spend the day doing something you love?

Wild fantasies, you say? Not for people who know what they want. Not for people who know how much is enough. Not for people who are more interested in satisfying their wants than they are in keeping up with their neighbors.

People who love what they do never <u>have</u> to go to work. They <u>want</u> to go to work. They want to go to work because they know how working and earning a living satisfies their wants.

Do you <u>have</u> to go to work every day? Do you know how much you have to earn to satisfy your wants? If not, there is only one person who can determine what will be enough for you. There is only one person who knows what you love to do.

***

The concept of attraction brings you what you want when you express those wants through your thoughts, vibrations and actions. If you have not clearly defined what you want, you will never satisfy your wants. All you will attract is a never-ending need for…more.

Decide what you want in life. Decide what makes you feel good. Decide what is enough for you to be happy. Then, you can begin to attract those things into your life.

4
The Role of the Subconscious Mind in Attracting the Life You Want

Because we don't think with our subconscious minds, we often don't think about our subconscious and the role it plays in our lives. While it appears our conscious minds attract what we want, it is our subconscious mind that wields the real power.

Research shows that our conscious minds are linear processors; that is, they only think about one thing at a time. In some ways that is good. When we focus our conscious mind on one subject, we are very powerful and productive and can effectively accomplish the task at hand.

The other part of our mind is our subconscious. When you stop and think about your subconscious, you will find that it is an amazing processor of information. Let me give you a couple of examples of the power of your subconscious mind and the role it plays in your life.

Have you ever wondered why you don't fall out of bed at night? When you are asleep, you obviously are not thinking about staying on the bed. That is your subconscious at work. It is running all the time like the basic operating software in your computer.

Here's another example. If you have ever purchased a car, remember what happened in the few weeks or days right before you bought it. You thought about getting a car or trading in your old one. You narrowed down your choices as to the model, make, and color you wanted to get. Finally, you came to a clear decision and selected the car you wanted.

Now, here is my question. After you made your decision about the car you wanted, did you start seeing that car everywhere?

Most people do. Why? Our subconscious minds act like an information filter for the conscious mind. The subconscious processes a virtually infinite amount of information, every second and every minute of every day. Our subconscious minds are the ultimate in multi-tasking, or perhaps we should say multi-processing.

When you started 'thinking' about getting a new car, your conscious mind gave linear thought to which car you would like to buy. It weighed the pros and cons and eventually came to a decision. At that point, your subconscious received a message that said, *"Hey, when you see that car out in the world, please bring it to our conscious attention."*

The truth is, your subconscious had been seeing every car that was around you, every day. All makes, models, colors and sizes. But, your subconscious filtered that information out before it went to your 'conscious' mind. Once your subconscious received the message that you were interested in a particular car, whenever it saw that car in the future, it passed that information on to your conscious mind.

This is a wonderful system. If your subconscious was not constantly filtering out all that unneeded information, your one-topic-processing-at-a-time conscious mind would quickly become overloaded.

Here's another example of your subconscious at work. Have you ever left your house, gotten into your car, started driving to work, the store, or an appointment, and, ten minutes later found yourself at that desired location…without consciously remembering a moment of the trip?

Many people have experienced this. It even has a name… daydreaming. When you think about it, it's pretty scary. Just consider (consciously) the enormous amount of information you must process to drive a car five to ten miles in busy city traffic. Cars, pedestrians, stop lights, relative speeds, cars changing lanes, drivers stopping suddenly in front of you.

Despite all the information that needed to be processed, you arrived safe and sound at your destination. Your subconscious processed all that information simultaneously, with enough leftover processing power for you to take a drink of coffee and sing to the song on the radio at the same time. Awesome!

Your subconscious mind is the real powerhouse of your information processing system. It is like the base operating software in your computer, running all the time, 24/7/365, never resting, always vigilant to your needs. It keeps you safe and snug <u>on</u> your bed every night, while your conscious mind is resting.

As wonderful as our subconscious minds are at processing information, however, they are only effective at processing what they have been told to do, just like your computer. Your conscious mind decides what you want and what needs to be done. Once you have 'made up your mind' (consciously), the subconscious joins in, processing all the information it receives, and helping the conscious mind to focus on the information needed to accomplish the task.

When you have made your decision, you must send consistent, accurate information to your subconscious so it understands where you want to go, and what you want to do, accomplish, and attract.

<u>It is not the job of your subconscious to make decisions about what you want.</u> It only processes information in support of the decisions your conscious mind makes.

It is also important to note that <u>your subconscious only operates on the last set of instructions it was given</u>. Those instructions cover every aspect of your life. Either consciously, or by default, you have given your subconscious a set of operating instructions related to driving a car, what foods you like to eat, what people you like to be around, and what colors you prefer.

Your subconscious has instructions about what you want in regard to sex, sports, religion, politics, work, play, entertainment, fun, garbage, mountains, tornadoes, and your friend or spouse. <u>You cannot give your subconscious too many instructions.</u>

You can, however, give it contradictory instructions. Just for fun, imagine that your subconscious is like a department in a company that is *'You, Inc.'* There is a foreman in your subconscious who oversees all its work. Can't you just imagine the following speech by the foreman of your Subconscious Processing Department?

***

Foreman to his staff:

"Good morning everyone of the morning crew. I hope you are all feeling well. It seems that the night crew was able to keep us on the bed, so now it is our turn to keep this company running smoothly.

"Unfortunately, the boys up in Consciousness have been thinking again. Sometimes I wish they would stop thinking so much. They are so inconsistent and always coming up with new, hare-brained ideas.

"Anyway, yesterday they read that book that we were told to bring to their attention, the one about the concept of Attraction. I don't know what it's about, but they seem to be all excited about it. After reading it, they have come up with some new operating instructions related to getting what 'we' want out of life.

"Yes, I know. This is not the first time they have addressed this issue. Seems like we get a new set of instructions every month or so on this topic. I don't know why the Consciousness group has so much trouble making up our mind. For crying out loud, they only have to think about one lousy thing at a time, while we have to filter through all the information that we see, feel, hear, touch, and smell during the day. We even have to keep things running smoothly at night while the Consciousness group gets its beauty sleep.

"Ah, well. As we know, 'Ours is not to reason why.' So, the specific area we are supposed to work on is the 'I want' programming.

"Now, as you know, we have been keeping the 'I want' program running smoothly for a long time. While it gets an occasional glitch now and again, most of our work on it has been maintenance-oriented since the basic instructions have not changed in years…many, many years.

"There are, unfortunately, thousands of instructions related to the 'I want' program. In fact, it is hard to think of an area that the 'I want' program doesn't affect. I wonder if the Consciousness group has any idea of the breadth and depth of the change they are requesting. We have been working on this program for years. I hope they know it is going to take time to implement the new instructions across all our systems.

"Anyway, let's get down to the specifics of the change. The current version of the 'I want' program uses the tried and proven 'I want, but' syntax. Some simple examples include:

- *"I want to change jobs, but I'm afraid to leave."*
- *"I want to have a better relationship, but I am not pretty enough to attract the person I think I want.*
- *"I want a new car, but I can't afford to buy one."*

"To be honest, I never understood the logic of those instructions. The first part always outlines a desire for something. Unfortunately, the 'but' always cancels out any action to be taken. So, the 'I want but' program just runs in an endless loop of non-action.

"The new language that we are to implement is 'I want <u>and</u>...' Now this makes a heck of a lot more sense. We know what we want and what action to take to get it. Funny, it just feels right.

"Oooops. My mistake. 'Feeling' is not our area. We have to leave that to the folks over in the Emotions and Feelings Department.

"Anyway, I hope the Consciousness Group sticks with this set of instructions for a while. It will make us more productive, and maybe even a little happier. So, let's get to work."

***

I think a conversation similar to this has been going on in my Subconscious Processing Department for longer than I care to admit. But now as I work to make sure that my conscious and my subconscious are working toward the same set of goals, I feel a lot better. At least, that's what the guys in my Emotions and Feelings Department tell me, and it's their job to know.

Now that we have a better understanding of the important and powerful role that the subconscious plays in attracting what we want, what can we do to make sure our whole team is operating on one set of instructions? <u>Produce a well-defined, well-thought-out set of instructions, goals, decisions, and wants.</u> We must also be sure to phrase our wants as something we are moving towards, with no 'buts' to get us stuck in an endless loop of the past.

As the foreman of the Subconscious Processing Department so accurately noted, most of us have been perfecting our *'I want but'*...program for a long time. We can expect it to take some time to change all that old programming to the new *'I want and'* syntax. However, once we implement the changes, once the new wording is in place, it will be easier and easier to plug that new syntax into more and more programs.

As we re-orient our thinking to what we want, we will attract more of what we want. As we notice that we are attracting more of want we want, we will then focus even more on what we want, with the Emotions and Feelings Department giving us continuous feedback about what feels good and what doesn't.

The beauty of this concept is that it is a simple system. We need to get all of our departments focused on the same set of clearly defined instructions, and then use our feelings to tell us when we are on course. If it feels good, all our departments are working together. If things don't feel good, we are out of sync with our desired programming and we need to refocus ourselves to get back on track.

***

Give your subconscious a clear set of well-defined instructions to follow and it will help you attract the life you want.

5
Three Things that Keep You from Attracting the Life You Want

As I talk with people about their efforts to attract good things into their lives, a number of thoughts, emotions and vibrations frequently show up in the process. I would like to briefly touch on three of these issues so that you might consider if they are negatively impacting your ability to attract the life you want.

Issue #1: I'm not good enough

Among the people who are consciously working at getting their 'It' together, I find many who have a stigma attached to themselves. Many of them feel that they are not, and will never be, 'good enough.' Many seem to be burdened with a belief that they are unworthy and do not deserve to be happy.

One reason why so many of us feel that we are not enough, and that we may never be enough, is that we always measure ourselves against other people and how we think they see us. Because of this predilection to see ourselves from someone else's viewpoint, it is important that we face a few facts related to this issue.

Many feelings of inadequacy have been created by the simple words and actions of others, especially when we were young. For example, many children are encouraged to believe in Santa Claus. Unfortunately, they are also taught that Santa keeps a list of 'good boys and girls' as a way of determining who gets presents at Christmas. If you came from a family that couldn't afford many presents during the holiday season, you might start to believe that you are a 'bad' person since Santa didn't bring you much.

We are affected by the words and actions of parents, relatives, elders, and peers. When Aunt Sally says *"You'll never be as smart as your sister,"* you end up feeling that you will never be good enough. Period. When your best friend tells you *"You're not sexy enough to get that guy or girl,"* you can carry that kind of mistaken belief with you for years, and allow it to stop you from going after what you really want in life.

As adults, we too often use the beliefs and opinions of others to tell us whether we are 'good enough.' The truth is, it should be totally irrelevant to you what others believe. It does no good to blindly accept the beliefs or opinions of others. The only reason for you to believe in the Tooth Fairy, UFO's, Elvis or 'The Almighty Dollar,' is if it makes you feel good.

Whether you choose to believe in something only matters if it makes you feel better. If you are a person who derives great joy and satisfaction from certain beliefs, then that is great. Don't let my beliefs or the beliefs of anyone else determine what makes you feel good.

Having said that, if you were hooked up to a lie detector and I asked you if you feel that you are now, or ever will be, 'good enough', what would your answer be? What is it that you feel when you think about that question? Does it bring great happiness and good feelings to mind, or does part of you want to go hide in hopes that no one will find out how you really feel?

For the moment, it's okay if you don't feel like you will ever be good enough. Lots of us have felt that way. It can often feel like no matter how hard we try, no matter how good we try to be, we always seem to be disappointing either ourselves or someone we know and love. The question is, if that is the way you feel in your heart and soul, what do you think that feeling will attract into your life? According to the concept of attraction, you will simply attract more disappointment.

We each have our own unique frequency. No two people vibrate at the same frequency. Thus, no matter how hard we try, we can never adjust our frequency to perfectly meet the needs and vibrations of someone else.

When you think of the people in your life who are important to you, do you want them to create static in their lives in a doomed attempt to match your frequency and make you happy? No, of course, you don't. You want them to be happy being who they are.

Well, if that is the way you feel about them, don't you think they feel the same way about you? People who <u>really</u> care about us just want us to be happy. In their hearts, they want us to accept ourselves for who we are, and to accept them the same way. They don't want us to have to change to meet their needs anymore than they want to have to change to meet ours.

The trouble is that most of us try so hard to be what we think others want us to be that we lose touch with our own pure vibration. We try so hard to vibrate in a way that will meet what we believe are the needs of others, that none of us maintain our own pure vibration. If we accept the fact that we can never tune our vibrations to perfectly match the vibrations of those we love, we can accept the fact that the best we can offer them (and ourselves) is to vibrate on our own clear frequency.

We are only enough for others when we are enough for ourselves.

As you may recall in Chapter 3, the definition of 'enough' is *"adequate for the want or need; sufficient for the purpose or to satisfy desire."* The only person who can determine what is enough for you is you. The way you determine what is enough is to decide what you want in life. Once you determine what you want, you are then in a position to focus your thoughts, your actions and your vibrations on attracting it.

It's simple. When we decide what we want and focus our intentions on the journey toward our wants, we have all we need to make us feel good in our lives. If you felt good most of the time about most aspects of your life, would that be enough? And, if you felt good most of the time, do you think that those you love would generally find you to be…more than enough to meet their needs? I think the answer is "Yes".

While it may take some time to understand who we are and to clear the static out of our systems, the truth is, not only are we good enough, we are perfect. Always have been, always will be.

We only 'think' of ourselves as being imperfect when we allow the words and actions of others to create static in our vibrations. Your perfection is always within you. All you have to do is clear out the static and get back to being who you are…a perfectly fine human being.

Issue #2: I'll never Fit In

This issue is closely related to Issue #1, but it has a slightly different feel to it. It is interesting that part of who we are wants to feel unique, to feel that we are special and unlike anyone else. But then there is another part of us that wants to 'fit in' with the world and the people around us. Part of us wants to belong and be accepted by others, and to be seen as being, well,...good enough.

Children in kindergarten know about wanting to fit in. So do adolescents and teenagers. The truth is, many of us carry that desire into adulthood. We want to be a part of something. We want to be accepted...preferably for just being who we are. Unfortunately, we may find ourselves in situations and places where there aren't many people around who share our interests and vibrations. We may find ourselves believing we have to conform to be able to fit in. Therein lies the problem.

If in the process of trying to conform we go against our natural vibrations, we set ourselves up to be miserable. While we might conform enough to 'fit in', we do so at the expense of giving up our natural frequencies and allowing static to create discord in our vibrations. The harder we try to fit in, the more static we emit. Eventually, our static speaks louder than our inner self and nobody wants us around.

As adults, we have enough life experience and the opportunity to make our own choices. We also have the responsibility to consciously choose the things that are most in concert and harmony with our natural vibrations. Otherwise, we are just contributing to the static of an unconscious and unfocused world.

One way to fit in with others is to emit clear vibrations that tell others who we are and what we want, and then to put our intentions, beliefs and actions into attracting others who will feel good in the presence of those vibrations. Trying to change our vibrations or the vibrations of those around us to make them match our own never works. How could it? The mere act of trying just creates more static. It is a never-ending battle that can only end in sadness.

If you feel the need to fit in with others, focus your attention on attracting people with similar vibrations. Move toward those whose vibrations feel good, and move away from those that don't. You will only feel like you really fit in (and feel good about it) when you are with others who are in harmony with your own natural vibrations.

Issue #3: Feeling Guilty

Have you ever felt guilty about something you said or did? What was it that you did that made you feel that way? Think of an instance when you felt really guilty about something and bring the situation into clear focus.

What happened that made you feel guilty? Did you promise to do something and fail to do it? Did you promise to be better or improve at something and then fail to follow through? Did you intentionally do something that you knew would hurt someone, and then felt badly after they were, in fact, hurt by what you did?

If you are honest with yourself in looking at these past situations, you may find that the feeling of guilt was created when you put yourself into a position of having to do something you didn't want to do. In many of those situations, you went against your natural feelings, vibrations and emotions, and forced yourself to do something that didn't feel good.

Why is that important? It is important because, at least some of the feelings of guilt that we experience are feelings of disappointment…in ourselves. We experience disappointment when we don't pay attention to our own wants, and we commit to something we don't want to do. Thus, many times we feel guilty because we don't pay attention to our personal wants.

The act of feeling guilty packs a triple whammy. (For those of you who are not familiar with the word 'whammy', it is a technical term meaning *'you are about to be kicked in the teeth hard enough to make your butt fall off.'*)

Why is feeling guilty a triple whammy? Well, the first whammy happens when you ignore your natural feelings and do something against your basic wants. This never feels good.

The second whammy happens when you spend time feeling guilty about agreeing to the situation that caused the first whammy.

And, finally, the third whammy happens when you feel guilty for having wasted time in the second whammy feeling guilty about the first whammy. Do you see a vicious cycle developing here? Once you get that snowball of guilt rolling, it picks up speed and power with each successive turn.

How do we avoid this avalanche of guilt? It is rather simple, although not always easy. One way to avoid guilt is to decide what you want, and then to avoid doing things that are not in vibration with those wants. By doing this, you don't feel guilty because you haven't gone against your natural wants (whammy #1.) Without whammy #1, there is no whammy #2. And, without whammy #2, there can be no whammy #3.

Yes, I realize that life is not always as simple as this. But that doesn't mean that we shouldn't focus our attention on avoiding whammies as much as possible. With that in mind, I would like to offer you one thing you can do that may help you keep from getting kicked in the teeth.

Learn to say *"No"*.

Wow! That was simple, don't you think? But, it is true. If you want to avoid feeling guilty and suffering the pain of triple whammies, learn to say *"No"* with a happy, natural confidence when that is what is necessary to stay true to your personal vibrations.

Question: *"Would you like to babysit our dog while we're on vacation?"*

Answer: *"Sorry, but I'm already watching my mother-in-law that weekend and that's enough whammies for one month."*

Question: *"Would you like to volunteer to manage the cheerleading squad during football games?"*

Answer: *"Gosh, thanks for the offer, but I'm already in charge of picking up the crap dropped by the mascot."*

Question: *"Would you like to have a double hernia operation to fix that cracked filling in your tooth?"*

Answer: *"Boy, that sounds like a great deal, but I think I'll have to wait until the cows come home to Capistrano before I would feel right about accepting such a generous offer."*

Yeah, yeah, I know. <u>You</u> would never be stupid enough to say *"Yes"* to such things, now would you? Well, don't look now, but you are about to get a whammy for lying through the teeth you soon won't have.

***

Face it. We're only human. We sometimes commit to stuff before our brains are fully engaged. To keep this from happening too often, remember this one simple rule: unconscious thinking leads to whammies. Keep that in mind the next time someone asks you to do something you really, really, really don't want to do. Your teeth and your butt will be eternally grateful.

6
Documenting What We Want

One of the reasons why people don't get what they want is because they don't know what they want. They haven't taken the time or made the effort to really think and feel what they want in life, and to direct their attention on attracting those things.

There is a second problem we can encounter when working toward what we want. For many of us, even when we have done a decent job of deciding what we want, most of us fail to write our wants down so that we can keep a clear focus on them as we move into the future.

Many self-help guides suggest that you write down your wants on paper. Now, I'll be honest, I personally dislike having to fill out worksheets or having to write that kind of stuff down in a journal or diary.

However, having said that, I also know that there are real benefits to documenting our wants on paper. Let me tell you a couple of these benefits as a way to encourage you (and myself!) to write your wants down even though you may not be thrilled about doing it.

Many of us feel that we don't need to write things down on paper as we believe we are quite capable of remembering our wants. Unfortunately, in practice, remembering our wants over weeks, months, and years can be difficult. When we try to remember our wants without writing them down, the following things tend to happen:

- We forget some important things completely.

- We forget the exact wording that seemed so powerful and energizing when we first came up with it.

- We fool ourselves into remembering our wants in words that fit...<u>how things turned out</u>. We tend to remember our wants in details that conveniently fit the result. Thus, we don't really know whether the results satisfied the original wants we were seeking to attract.

- When we don't keep our written wants in a place that is easily accessible, we seldom refer to them as we make decisions in our lives.

On the other side of the ledger, a number of positive things tend to happen when we actually put our thoughts and desires in writing:

- Research has shown that some people learn information auditorally, some learn visually, and others learn kinesthetically. By writing our wants down on paper, we invoke two forms of learning... visual and kinesthetic. By doing both, we send two different forms of messages to our Subconscious Processing Departments, two ways of reinforcing the '*I want and*' <u>program</u>.

(If we really want to embed our wants into our subconscious, we can also read our list out loud. This ensures we have used all three primary ways to communicate to our subconscious.)

- By having our wants written on a piece of paper (or typed on a computer and then printed), they have a physical substance to them as opposed to just being nerve impulses shooting around in our heads. They become more real, more tangible; something we can actually hold in our hands. Having taken on substance, it is easier to review, support, and act upon them as we move through life.

- When carried in written form in our wallet or purse, they are readily available to guide us when we make important decisions. A quick review of our list allows us to make decisions that are consistent with our wants. Taking that extra moment to review our written wants can pay big dividends both in the present moment, and in the future.

If you find that you have trouble remembering your wants; if you have trouble keeping them clear in your mind; if you have difficulty consistently telling your conscious and subconscious minds what to focus on, consider writing your wants down on paper. Just a few words for each want is all that is necessary…just enough words so you can remember the good feeling associated with that want.

Keeping your list close at hand can also be a useful tool to help you get out of the muck of a bad-feeling situation. Remove yourself from the situation and then quietly read your list of wants over and over in your mind. Think about how good you feel when you are moving forward toward your desires.

***

Your conscious mind can only think about one thing at a time. If it is focused on reading your list of wants, it can't be wasting time dwelling in the past, worrying about the future, or getting stuck in the now.

7
Too Busy Being Busy

A friend of mine was telling me the other day about how unbelievably busy her life is. She juggles her career, family, school functions, church activities, volunteer work, Tai Chi class, a garage sale...and so on. I asked her if she was enjoying life in the midst of all this activity. Her response was honest and matter-of-fact:

"Are you kidding? I'm way too busy to have a life."

What a sad commentary on the state of a person's life! *"I'm too busy to have a life."* Yet, we hear people making the same or similar comments about their lives.

"I'd love to do that but I'm too busy."

"Sorry, can't go tonight; too busy."

"Maybe we can do it next year when we aren't so busy."

And the classic: *"I'm way too busy to take time off."*

We often say we don't have time to sit down and think about what we want. Too busy. Too busy being busy. Too busy being...miserable? Unfortunately, when we get lost in being busy, next year seldom looks any different than this year or last year.

What are we so busy doing that we don't have time, or won't make time, to attract the life we want? Is everything we are doing that important? I guess that depends on what we have decided is important. Maybe a more important question that must be asked first is: *"Have I consciously decided what I want?"*

Most of us don't get what we want in life because we don't <u>know</u> what we want. We haven't taken the time to really think and feel what we want. We haven't made a conscious decision about what we want. Are you one of those people? If you are, I guess you might take comfort in knowing you are not the only person who doesn't know what you want.

But, what I want you to think about...right now...is this: How can you ever hope to get what you want if you haven't <u>decided</u> what you want? How can you ever hope to put your thoughts, your energies, your passions, and your will behind attracting what you want if you don't know what that is?

The simple answer is...you are highly unlikely to <u>attract</u> what you want until you have decided <u>what</u> you want. Period. End of discussion. And anybody who tells you otherwise is a liar. It may seem a little harsh to have to think about life this way, but perhaps it's time we face some facts about what we must do to attract the life we want.

Let me ask you a riddle that relates to this issue. Three crows were sitting on a fence near a cornfield. Two crows decided to fly to the cornfield to feed. Question: How many crows were left sitting on the fence?

If your answer is zero, one or two...sorry, wrong answer.

The correct answer is three. Why? Because ***deciding*** to fly to the cornfield is not the same thing as ***flying*** to the cornfield.

Thinking about something and even deciding to do something accomplishes absolutely…NOTHING! It is only after we act upon our thoughts and decisions that something will happen.

"But, I am acting on my decisions," one crow said. "Can't you see how busy I am? How could I be this busy and not be attracting what I want?

"I mean, it sure seems like I should be moving toward what I want. I'm flapping my wings a hundred times a minute. Fact is, though, I'm getting pretty tired of flapping. And, I don't seem to be getting any closer to what I want. Maybe it would help if I let go of the fence."

"But, this is such a nice fence to sit on. Well, actually, come to think of it, it isn't really that great a fence. There are lots of splinters in it that hurt my feet and it hasn't been painted in years. The top rail where I used to sit has fallen down and now I have to sit on this lower rail."

"I guess I also hadn't noticed that the tree that used to shade the fence has fallen down. Man, it gets hot out here in the summer. And the wind blows like crazy across the field in winter. The snow blows so hard I can barely see my wing in front of my beak.

"But, hey, lots of crows don't have a fence as good as mine. Poor birds, having to live in trees and barns. Last week Charlie decided he was going to fly south this winter to live someplace warm. Funny, he said the same thing last year. Guess his job responsibilities are holding him back.

"Me, I like my fence. So what if the barn is warm in the winter, dry in the spring, and cool in the summer? This fence is the only life I know. My father sat on this very fence and so did his father. It's my lot in life to sit on this fence, isn't it?

"I mean, it's not like I'm a songbird or anything, flying around singing all day. Cheery little devils get on my nerves. I wish they'd go sing somewhere else. All those happy little songs make me sick.

"And, it's not like I'm a rooster, you know. Those guys get all the breaks. A nice condo to live in with a bunch of dames at your peck and call. All the ground corn you can eat. And all he has to do to earn his keep is to get up once a day at sunrise and go 'cock-a-doodle-doo.'

"No, I like it here on the fence. I can sit here all day and just watch the world go by."

Well, you get the idea. As simple as this example might seem, there are some very important points to take note of from our friend the crow.

- You can flap all you want (being busy), but you won't get anywhere unless you let go of the fence.

- If you don't fly over the hill, you will never get to the corn on the other side.

- Complaining about how good someone else's life seems to be won't do a darn thing to improve yours.

- Sitting on a fence allows you to watch the world go by, but your life may be passing you by, too.

Are you living your life like the crow? Are you acting on what you want? Have you really decided what you want? Or are you just sitting on the fence watching the world go by, hoping that something good will happen?

Much as we might like things to be otherwise, the truth is:

- You will never have the opportunity to get what you want if you don't decide what you want.

- Thinking about doing something and deciding to do something never actually accomplishes anything. It is only after you take action that something can change.

If you are always 'too busy being busy' to stop and decide what you want, and, if you never take action towards getting what you want, you will end up exhausted from flapping and no closer to your goals than you were yesterday.

***

When you notice that your feet hurt, you are cold and tired, your shoulders ache, and the world seems to be passing you by, you have to decide what you want to do. You have to decide to let go of the fence, and then allow yourself to fly toward your goals. Remember:

> "It is far better to be busy being,
> than to be busy being busy."

8
Navigating the River of Life

Many writers and philosophers use a river as a metaphor for life. We hear phrases like "swimming upstream against the current," "standing firm like a rock in the river," and "going with the flow." In many ways, living life is like navigating a river.

Swimming Upstream

There are many of us who have, at one time or another, struggled in an attempt to swim upstream against the current of life. These are the times when nothing seems to go right; when there never seems to be enough time or money; when relationships are fleeting, difficult, and unsatisfying.

Work is a pain. The kids are a pain. Life is a pain. It is a time when it is 'hard to keep one's head above water' against the flood of perceived misfortune that life sends us. Know the feeling? We all do. But, we can't just give up. That isn't the way big people deal with their problems. We tough it out and suck it up, whatever the pain.

Standing Firm Like a Rock in the River

Another way we navigate the 'River of Life' is to stand still and be like a rock in the middle of the river. Stand firm.

Don't budge. Fight the relentless pressure of the current until we get so tired we just can't fight anymore. Forget the fact that by standing in one place, we aren't actually getting anywhere. We end up stuck in the same old place, fighting the same old current day after day with no end in sight.

There we are, in the middle of the river, going nowhere. Not a place any of us want to be. But wait; it gets worse. While we are standing there, we form a barrier in the river and create a lot of turbulence and chaos for those around us. Bummer. Not exactly a way to make friends.

Going with the Flow

A third option that many people choose is to simply "go with the flow." That sounds pretty nice, doesn't it? No more fighting upstream against the current. No more pushing like a rock against the never-ending pressure, and no more creating chaos all around. Just go with the flow.

While this may be a better option than swimming upstream or standing like a rock, this option seldom brings any satisfaction to those who try it. Why?

In truth, 'going with the flow' lets the river decide where we go and where we end up. We don't decide what we want or where we want to go. Not surprisingly, we often end up being disappointed with the results of our 'non-actions'. When we go with the flow, we relinquish our personal responsibility and let life lead us.

What is true about all three of these options is that none of them get us closer to what we wanted, closer to where we wanted to go. In options one and two, we don't go anywhere. In option three, we end up wherever the river happens to take us. None of these are active choices. They are choices by default without any input from us.

Two other options

Now let's look at the concept of the River of Life from a different angle. We can stop fighting the river and make the river work for us rather than against us. These ideas work well with the concept of attraction.

A river is defined as moving water traveling downstream between two banks. One option we might consider when we are tired of swimming upstream or tired of standing fast against the current is to simply crawl out on the bank and rest for a while.

It appears that many people have either (1) never thought of this as an option, or (2) they were told that it was not allowed. *"Stay in there and fight. Don't be a loser. Don't be a pansy. Hang in there and tough it out!"*

What a bunch of malarkey that is! It is my belief that it is fine to climb out on the bank occasionally and rest when the River of Life is too turbulent. Get out of the rat race; re-evaluate our list of wants. Determine where <u>we</u> want to go when we head downstream. In that way, we will be navigating, not just going with the flow to unknown and possibly unwanted places.

Now, while it may be all right to get out on the bank and rest, the truth is, until we get back into the river, we will never get closer to what we want. Until we get back into the flow, we are just bystanders, watching the River of Life pass us by.

The River of Life teems with opportunity as it flows downstream. This is important to note because, contrary to what some people might think, many of the things we think we have missed come around again if we want them. At no point in our journey has life completely 'passed us by.'

Remember, we will never get to where we want to go unless we determine where that place is. Once we do that, we must get back into the flow of the River of Life and use its power to take us there. <u>We are each responsible for plotting the course that will achieve our wants.</u>

No one else can navigate the river for us. We can ask others for advice about the perils and opportunities in the River of Life, but ultimately, we are the only ones who steer our lives. If we follow the directions of others, we will just end up in places <u>they</u> wanted to go.

***

When you are tired of swimming upstream against the current; tired of standing firm against life as it swirls around you; tired of going with the flow to the wrong destinations; it's okay to crawl out onto the bank and rest for awhile. It's okay to take a little time to review your list of wants and focus on attracting them into your life. And, then, when you put your thoughts, beliefs, and actions into attracting the life you want, the River of Life will help transport you on your journey.

9
We All Come from Dysfunctional Families

Do you ever feel like you came from a dysfunctional family? Yeah, me too. And so do most other people I talk with. The more I thought about this, the more I realized that <u>we all come from dysfunctional families</u>. The only question is, what was the particular dysfunctional area in your family?

Now, some people say: *"I don't think children who are born into wealthy families or smart families have to suffer from the same kinds of problems I had to deal with in my childhood."*

My response to that statement would be, *"You're right."* Children from those kinds of families probably don't have to deal with the same problems as children from other families. However, that does not mean that wealthy and smart families do not have problems.

Most of us can identify aspects of our families that could be called dysfunctional. Some families have issues with money. Others have issues with relatives. Some families have problems related to sex, while others let work get in the way of life.

As children, we may have also felt burdened by an endless list of traits that made us feel dysfunctional compared to our peers. Some children feel they are not smart enough and suffer because of it. Others are smart and therefore feel that they <u>have</u> to make straight A's on every report card to be worthy.

We all have issues and occasionally feel insecure. We can feel inadequate like Sue, who feels she is not as pretty as her friend Ellen. Sue lacks confidence and blames her lack of friends on her plain appearance. But, Ellen has her own concerns. She believes that her mother only loves her <u>because</u> she is pretty. Ellen feels that she will have to maintain her looks forever or her mother (and all the other people in Ellen's life) will not love her.

Families have dysfunctions related to abuse, addictions, co-dependency, politics, religion, sex, money, in-laws, work; well, you get the idea. Simply take heart in knowing that you are not the only person who came from a family that was not the model for the Cleavers in *"Leave It to Beaver."*

What does this have to do with attracting the life you want? Regardless of how dysfunctional your family was, you still turned out surprisingly well. You are probably a relatively decent person. Maybe you aren't Mother Teresa, but you didn't end up being a serial killer either. Therefore, one can only conclude that you have attracted some good things into your life. You have also attracted things that helped you define who you are and who you want to be.

Let's not forget that we're only human. We come equipped with all kinds of interesting traits and beliefs and issues. <u>We come with our own unique vibration and frequency.</u> As children, we get all kinds of static (and harmony) laid onto our vibrations by our parents and elders. Why did we attract that particular set of parents? Heck, I don't know. We just did.

Our families and friends and the people around us help us learn who we are and what we want. My wife says that we have children so that they can teach us everything we need to know. This may well be true because, as Robert Fulghum so aptly stated: *"All I really need to know I learned in kindergarten."*

GETTING YOUR 'IT' TOGETHER

If you suffered from physical, mental or emotional pain because of dysfunctional people in your life, I'm sorry that those things had a negative impact on your past. But, <u>you are the only person who can make sure that the rest of your life is better</u>. You have the power to create a life that feels good... a life spent doing what you love, with people who love you, people who respect you, and people who accept you for who you are.

***

Whatever dysfunctional influences you may have had in your life, you now have a choice. Are you going to let the static of dysfunctional influences affect your life? Or are you going to focus your thoughts, your energy and your vibrations to attract the life you want? You have the choice and the opportunity. It's your decision.

10
The Vibrations of Words

In writing this book, I use words to convey information, ideas, concepts, and feelings that you can use to improve the quality of your life. Unfortunately, in a book, the only way I can do that is through the use of words (yes, pictures can also help tell the story. But, in this book, I will use words to convey my point.)

Did you ever stop to think about the fact that words have vibrations attached to them? Our eyes sense the vibrations of the way words look. Our ears sense the way words sound. Words can evoke our senses of smell, taste and touch through their vibrations. The vibrations of words can affect us on mental, emotional and spiritual levels.

Unfortunately, we may have become too dependent upon words in our technologically-driven world. We rely on words to tell a story on TV, the radio, on CD's and DVD's, in magazines, newspapers, online articles, and dozens of other ways. And, for some reason, we implicitly trust that the words we hear or read tell an accurate story.

There is an old saying that goes:

> "I know you believe you understand what you think I said, but I'm not sure you realize that what you heard is not what I meant."

While words can be very powerful in conveying information, different words mean different things to different people. Thus, as the saying so aptly states, what you think you heard may not be what I meant.

One of the things I have noticed about words is that people often have trouble relating to certain words. My own experience is that there are words with which I don't have much of a relationship. One of those words is 'feel'.

In discussions with my wife (at times when we weren't necessarily communicating well on the same vibrational wavelengths), she would sometimes ask me, "*Well, how does that feel?*" Over the years I found that I would often answer her based on what I 'thought' about the issue, not on how I felt about the issue.

Thus, even the word 'feel' has a different vibration for some people versus others. For those who are more kinesthetically-oriented, they can actually feel the word 'feel' in their bodies. For those of us who tend to come more from a 'thinking' place, the word 'feel' may not have much of a 'feeling' to it at all.

What does this have to do with living a better life and using attraction to get what you want in life?

We have been told by many different philosophers that paying attention to our feelings is a good way to determine whether we are doing what we like, and to determine whether we are vibrating our frequency clearly, without much static. If it feels good, we are on the right path. If it feels bad, we have gotten off the trail and we need to refocus our thoughts, energies, and actions back in the desired direction.

But what if a person doesn't know what feeling good feels like? Let me show you how the words we use to 'think' about what we want, can energize or inhibit us from getting us what we want, and from getting us to where we want to go.

For a moment, I would like you to consider the word 'want'. How does the word 'want' make you 'feel'?

When you think of the word want, as in *"I want to have a new car,"* does this produce a feeling like you have a new car, or a feeling of a lack of having a new car? While this may sound like a silly question, according to the concept of attraction, how you feel about the word 'want' is very important in determining whether you will, in fact, attract what you want.

In talking to people about what they want, I have noticed that many (if not most) of us have a vibration of *'I don't have'* attached to the word 'want'. If we want something, the primary reason we want it is because we <u>don't</u> have it. We come from a feeling of lack, as opposed to having a feeling of enjoyment generated by the thought of how it would feel if we did have it.

Unfortunately, we cannot attract what we want by saying what we 'don't' want. When we use words like 'not' or 'no' or 'don't' or 'can't', our systems vibrate with the negative words. *"I don't want that"* translates into a vibration of *"I want that."* When we make a statement from a position of what we don't want, attraction ignores the 'don't', and, therefore, we attract that which we don't want.

Similarly, when we say "I want something," if in our minds we are actually saying "I want that...because I don't have it," we will simply attract more 'not having'.

I have talked to people who believe they have been working with honesty, sincerity and passion to use the concept of attraction in their lives. But, many of them say, *"I just seem to keep getting what I don't want, even though I have phrased my words in the form of 'I want.'"*

This is where the vibrations of words come into play. Even though we may use the words 'I want', because many of us associate the word 'want' with 'not having', the vibration we send out is one of not having. When we vibrate not having, attraction brings us more not having.

> **Attraction does not respond to words.
> It responds to the vibrations associated with the words.**

The concept of attraction responds to the vibrations and feelings you associate with the words. If the words mean one thing to the 'thinking' you but something very different on a vibratory level to the 'feeling' you, <u>you will attract what you feel</u>, not what you think.

This is tricky stuff. If there is any truth to this concept of attraction, we must give attention to using words that create the vibration of what we want to attract. Let me give an example.

"I want to have enough money to have the things I want and to feel free."

For many people, this statement may be just fine on a vibratory level to attract more money and the freedom that having more money provides. But, for others, because they 'want' more money, and because they feel that they don't have enough, this statement will attract 'not having enough money.'

I have found that many words put my attention on the past. *"I want money…because I don't have money and have never had enough money."* (This is a 'past' orientation). How might this statement be rephrased to produce the vibration of attracting more money?

I have experimented with different wording to produce a feeling of <u>having</u> money. When I use words that convey a sense of forward movement toward my goal, I don't have those same old feelings that were anchored in the past.

Some of the phrases I have found useful include:

"I am moving forward toward my goal of having enough money."

"I am approaching the point where I have enough money."

"I am well on my way to having all the money I want."

With these phrases, I no longer feel held down by the 'not having' of the past. These phrases convey movement toward something or someplace, like leaving on a trip and driving toward a destination.

The concept of attraction allows us to attract what we want. If we look at attracting what we want as though we were taking a trip, we will not get to our destination until the very end of the trip. In the meantime, we aim ourselves in the direction of our destination, and we put our thoughts, energies and beliefs into the thought that if we keep moving <u>forward</u> on this heading, we will eventually get to our destination.

Unfortunately, we live in a world that seeks instant gratification. We want to get there and we want to get there right now!

Let's assume we want a new car that costs $25,000. But, we only have $5,000. Thus, we need to attract $20,000 more before we can get our car.

By putting our thoughts and energies and actions behind our desire to have that car, we can attract the other $20,000.

However, it may not come all at once. We might get $500 this month, and $1,000 next month, and maybe $10,000 the month after.

From one perspective, the old view of *"I <u>don't</u> have a new car,"* we still don't have our new car. Thus, that is the vibration we emit; which, of course, means…we will not get our new car.

If, on the other hand, we see that we have made $11,500 worth of progress towards the $20,000 more that we need, we will feel good about getting closer to our goal. The closer we get, the more we believe we can get there, which attracts more money, and gets us even closer to our goal.

Whatever it is that we want; whatever it is that we want to do in our lives; the truth is, where we are now is simply the starting point on the road to the future. While our past has brought us to this point, no amount of thinking about that past and how we haven't gotten what we want will ever help us get where we really want to go.

***

If we continue to use words to convey our feelings, and if those feelings come from the feelings of lack that we experienced in the past, we will find ourselves there, surrounded by lack, in the future. When you pick words and phrases to describe what you want, use words that have a feeling of movement toward what you want. Don't use words that keep you anchored to a past you don't like.

Then, put your thoughts, energies, and actions behind those words with passion and gusto, as if you could see your destination on the horizon. Soon you will find yourself making forward progress, and feeling better about the journey.

11
You Only Feel Bad If You Think You Do

Of the many concepts that I present in this book to help you improve the quality of your life, the idea that you only feel bad if you think you do generates the most controversy and debate. That said, let me take a moment to reiterate what I hope to accomplish in this book.

You do not have to agree with any of the ideas I put forward. I offer them only as a catalyst to help you determine how you can direct your life to attract what you want. Thus, when I make a statement like *"You only feel bad if you think you do"*, I make that statement purely to get you to notice when it is that you feel bad (or good).

I believe that we attract what we focus our intentions and feelings on. In order to attract what we want, we must know how we feel at any given moment. But how do we <u>know</u> what we feel? And where do we sense what we feel? As a way for you to experience this for yourself, I would like for you to conduct a simple thought experiment.

Imagine that a very close friend or loved one is standing right in front of you. Once you have that image in mind, I will ask you to do something. Immediately after you do what I tell you, I want you to notice what, where, and how you feel in your body.

Close your eyes and imagine that person standing right in front of you. Now, I want you to slap that person as hard as you can right across the face. How do you feel?

Because this a person we like/love, when we think about having slapped this person very hard across their face, most of us will experience a bad physical feeling somewhere in our body.

Did you notice a feeling? Where is the feeling? What does it feel like?

Now, some people who do this experiment may not feel anything. And, they will think that it is 'bad' that they didn't feel anything. *"I didn't feel anything so I must be a bad, un-feeling person."*

If you are one of those people, here is the good news. When you had that thought that you were a 'bad' person for not noticing a different feeling…you felt bad about that! If you did, notice how and where you had that bad feeling. At this point, we don't care how it is that you came to have the bad feeling, only that you experienced a bad feeling somewhere in your system.

Now, I want you to picture this person you like/love standing right in front of you again. But, this time, I want you to give this person a big hug. How does that feel?

For most people, the feeling you have in your body when you give a hug will feel better than the feeling you had when you slapped the person. That is the simple first step to understanding our feelings…being able to compare what feels bad to something that feels better. When we can notice those differences, we can use them to guide us toward more of what feels good.

As interesting as that little experiment might have been, I want to make a point that is much more important than the experiment.

The truth is, in the reality of the world in which we live, that person was not standing in front of you and you did not slap or hug that person. Those images were purely in your mind. However, <u>the feelings you felt after you imagined slapping and hugging the person were just as real as if the person had actually been there!</u>

But, how can that be? We know in our minds that the experiment wasn't real, yet we felt real feelings anyway, just as real as if the situation had actually happened. The truth is, if the mind 'thinks' that we are feeling something, we feel it. If the mind 'thinks' we are not feeling something, we don't.

The old saying, *"It's all in your mind"* may have a lot more truth to it than we realize. When something is *'all in our mind,'* it is not necessarily a bad thing. It is bad only if we believe it is bad.

How does this help us improve the quality of our lives and learn how to attract the kind of life we want? Our ability to attract things into our lives is based on the feelings and vibrations we emit, not just the words we use or the thoughts we have. However, our minds play a large role in determining whether we think something feels good or not. If we believe something feels good, it does, and we will emit good vibrations because of it.

If the mind 'thinks' we feel bad, we are more likely to emit bad vibrations, and we will attract more bad feelings. What is more important is that the mind can <u>create</u> feelings (good or bad) just by thinking about them! Bad (and good) things don't have to actually happen in the 'real' world for us to feel them.

Thus, it is in our best interest to notice when something feels good, or at least to notice when we 'think' something feels good. When we 'think' that we feel good, we will attract more feeling good.

We get into trouble when our minds think one thing, but we feel something else. That inconsistency produces a lot of static in our systems. Static seldom makes us feel good. Learning to have our thoughts in sync with our feelings is vital if we are to emit vibrations that will attract what we really want.

There have been many people who have touched upon this idea. In the 1600's, Descartes said *"I think, therefore I am."* Henry Ford is quoted as having said, *"Whether you think you can, or think you can't, you'll be right."*

All of these words refer to the same idea. We are what we think we are. If that is true, and if we attract what is like us, then what we think we are is what we will attract. How we think we feel is how we feel.

Who do you think you are? Who do you think you want to be? What do you feel inside when you think about those things? Do you feel good when you think about changing jobs? Do you feel good when you think about finding a life-long friend?

How do you feel when you think about how poorly you may have been treated in the past? How do you feel when you bitch, moan, and complain about not having something? Can you start to get a 'feeling' as to why it is important to have our 'thinking' parts and our 'feeling' parts following the same plan?

What can we do to make sure that what we think, what we feel, and what we think we feel, are all aimed at the same wants? We must first think about what we want. When we think about something, we can notice how that thought feels. If it feels good, we want to think about it some more.

If we decide that something feels good, we can let our thoughts, our energy and our actions create harmonious vibrations that will attract more of the same.

We need to recognize that we are in control of what we think and feel. No one else can make us feel or think something unless we allow them to. And, no one else can determine when something feels good to us, because they will never have the same unique frequency we do.

***

You have the ability...and the responsibility...to create the world that you want by directing your thoughts, vibrations, actions and feelings toward that which...feels good. Why would you want to operate any other way?

12
Feeling Good by Not Feeling Bad

When I first read about the concept of attraction, I realized that I had spent a lot of time in the past not feeling good (mentally or emotionally). My focus had mostly been on the bad feelings of the past. Focusing on those bad feelings had often attracted more of the same.

I had forgotten what feeling good feels like. Even though I tried to move toward things that I 'thought' would feel good, did they really feel good, or was I just fooling myself into thinking they felt good?

About the same time I read about the concept of attraction, I came across a book entitled *"Addicted to Unhappiness"*. In this book, the authors said that as children, we can accidentally be taught to believe, through the words and actions of our parents, teachers and elders, that things that don't feel good are what feeling good was supposed to feel like.

An example concerned babies who were allowed to cry themselves to sleep (this was a parenting concept that was promoted and used on babies of the Baby Boomer generation). The theory was that by crying, the baby was trying to coerce/manipulate the parent into giving it constant attention, and that only by ignoring the crying would the baby learn to stand on its own and become self-reliant.

The authors of the *Unhappiness* book put forth a different idea. They hypothesized that when a baby cries, it is not feeling good about something. It is hungry, cold or wet; its surroundings are too loud; or any number of other reasons. A baby whose parents come to its aid learns that it feels better to have a dry diaper than a wet one. It learns that having a full tummy feels better than having an empty one. The baby learns that when the problem is taken care of, it feels good again.

Unfortunately, when parents do not respond to the needs of a crying baby, the baby learns an entirely different lesson.

Babies come into the world believing that their parents love them. They believe, without question, that their parents know what is best for them, and that their parents will only do what is best for them.

So, consider this picture. The baby has a wet diaper and starts crying because the wet diaper really doesn't feel good. The parents, however, do not change the baby, leaving it miserable. The baby still believes that its parents do only what is best for it, and comes to the conclusion that having a wet diaper must be a good thing. Therefore, the baby is taught to believe that the really bad feeling of a wet diaper…is what feeling good is supposed to feel like, no matter how bad it actually feels.

Of course, the baby's internal sensors still tell it that this cold wet diaper feels like, well,…like crap!

The authors' point is that we can end up being addicted to unhappiness because we have the grossly mistaken idea that feeling 'bad' in our wet diaper (a bad relationship, depression, fat, etc.) is what feeling good is **supposed** to feel like. We can unconsciously end up spending the rest of our lives seeking out bad feelings with the hope that at some point they will start to feel good.

Talk about a split personality. Whatever the cause, it is possible that some of us may have ended up with a distorted view and understanding of what 'feeling good' really feels like.

GETTING YOUR 'IT' TOGETHER

It is often difficult to know and trust what feels good to us. We may have become so confused trying to decide what feels good, that we have difficulty actually feeling what feels good. This situation makes it difficult for us to know what feels good, and to use our feelings to guide us toward what we want.

To attract what we want, we must know what we want. To do that, we must be able to determine what feels good without the overtones of the past getting in the way. But, breaking the habit of dwelling in the past is not easy.

I'm pleased to say that I don't dwell on the past nearly as much as I used to. I did this by learning to trust what feels good to me. Here was my thought process.

"I have not been happy re-living the past. I have been doing that for many years and I have more than ample proof that living in the past is not making me happy or getting me closer to what I want.

"Therefore, it only makes sense to try something different. While I may not know if living in the present or focusing on what I want in the future will work, I do know that focusing on the past doesn't work. In truth, the only hope or opportunity that I have to become happier and get more of what I want, is to actively focus on what I want to attract."

I came to the following conclusion:

If you dwell in the past, you will find yourself still living there in the future.

Every time I caught myself thinking about the past, I replaced that thought with a thought that focused on what I wanted:

"I feel good being safe, happy, healthy and prosperous."

That's it. I focused on that thought and said that statement out loud every time I found myself thinking, worrying, bitching, moaning, or complaining about the past, or about what I didn't have.

And you know what? I started feeling better. Did I feel 'good'? Well, I can't say that I necessarily felt like dancing in the streets or that I experienced wild euphoria. But, I did feel better than when I thought about and dwelt in the past.

I learned how to feel good by not feeling bad.

I don't know about you, but that was a huge step for me. I started feeling 'not bad.' That helped me get a better understanding, a better feeling, for what felt good. The more I did it, the better I felt. Within a month, I felt better mentally and emotionally than I had felt in years.

The wonderful thing about this concept is, when you make the shift away from the past and what you don't want, even if it is just for a moment or an hour or a day, you feel better for that amount of time. You don't just 'think' you feel better. You do feel better. And it feels good!

Since we attract what we feel, the more we feel good and the more we want to feel good, the more 'feel good' we attract. Thus, we start to re-train ourselves to go for the good feelings instead of wallowing in the bad ones.

If you are like me and you have spent a lot of your time complaining about the past, now is the time to stop. Create a statement that describes what you want. Don't worry if you can't feel the goodness or truth of the statement just yet. Just trust it. And every time you find yourself wallowing in the past, think and say your statement to yourself...every time.

At first, you may find yourself having to think and say your positive statement to yourself a hundred times or more a day. That's okay. Let's face the truth: It took us a whole lot of years to perfect our negative, living-in-the-past thoughts and behaviors. It is unlikely that we can turn that ocean liner of past thoughts around on a dime. Go easy on yourself. You're worth it!

Also, when you catch yourself thinking about the past, don't get down on yourself or feel guilty just because you have slipped back a little. Just repeat your positive statement. You may be surprised at how those thoughts about the past will become less important, less powerful, and will arise much less often.

Keep repeating your statement until you feel better. And, <u>when you start feeling better, pay attention to that feeling.</u> Glory in feeling better. That better/good feeling you have is what 'not feeling bad' feels like. Once you feel it a few times, I guarantee you will want to feel that way more, lots more.

After a few days, weeks or maybe a few months, you will find that you spend much less time dwelling in the past and much more time feeling better in the now. You will also find yourself wanting to feel good in the future. If you want it, if you put your feelings and desires and vibrations behind your wants, then that is what you will attract.

Oh, oh. What was that I just heard you say? Did I hear you say, *"That's fine for you, Hawkeye, but it will never work for me"?*

If you did think that, here is your first chance to think a better thought and stop living in the past. Do it right now.

If nothing else, read the following paragraph out loud a few times until you start feeling less bad.

I enjoy feeling happy, healthy and prosperous. I like feeling good. I want to go after those things that make me feel good. I like being around people who make me feel good. I like having a job that makes me feel good. I like the thought of having plenty of money in the bank so I can feel good and free.

Just keep saying that over and over and you know what? When you say it a few times, you <u>will</u> feel better. Now, I didn't promise that you would feel great. But I do promise that, if you allow yourself to feel the vibrations of these words, you <u>will</u> notice that you feel at least a little better than you did before you said those words.

How do I know that? Because it is a scientifically proven fact that your conscious mind can only think about one thing at a time. Therefore, during the time you are thinking about and saying those words, <u>you cannot be thinking about the past</u>. And that is the whole point of doing it.

We can start to learn how to feel good by not feeling bad. We can learn to feel better by thinking and saying good things right now.

<u>Feeling less bad is good</u>. It is a start. That is all most of us need…a small step on the path toward feeling better and focusing on what we want. If we can feel better for just a little while, and then focus on having and attracting that feeling more and more, we <u>will</u> feel better. The more we feel it, the more we attract it. The more we attract it, the more we feel it. Pretty soon, we have that ocean liner of past thoughts turned around and sailing in the direction of what feels good and what we want.

So, here is my question to you about this approach. If you are a person who tends to dwell in and on the past, how's that working for you? Are you happier than a bee in a honey factory? Or do you wallow in the bad feelings of the past? If the latter is your answer, then what have you got to lose by trying this idea?

It's doubtful that it will make you feel any worse than you did before you tried it. And, maybe, just maybe, there is a chance that it will make you feel better.

Ask yourself this question. How many hours did you feel good yesterday? Ten? Five? One? What? You didn't feel good at all? Well, if you spend five minutes today saying those positive statements to yourself, that will be five more minutes of feeling better today than you did yesterday. If you do it again tomorrow, that will be another five minutes of feeling better. Who knows? In a month or so you might feel better for an entire hour.

***

It doesn't matter whether you feel good five hours a day at present or five minutes. The only question you need to answer is whether you want to feel better for a longer period of time tomorrow than you did today. If so, give this a try. If it doesn't work, what have you lost? But, if it does work, even just a little bit, that short period of time spent feeling better could be the start you need toward…Getting Your 'It' Together.

13
Learning from Bad Feelings

A friend of mine asked me the other day if there is ever a situation where having a bad feeling was a good thing. While that might seem like a silly question, it isn't. In fact, there are probably many situations where a bad feeling is not only okay, it may even be necessary. A good example of this is the situation where someone close to us passes away.

Everything in the universe vibrates. The people we love and live with emit vibrations, and when we are nearby, we feel their vibrations. When someone close to us dies, a void is created in our vibrational lives.

It is similar to what happens when we turn off the radio. We hear (and often feel) the sound vibrations from the radio. When we turn the radio off, those vibrations stop and we sense the loss of that vibration. Thus, when someone close to us ceases to vibrate, we notice it. We feel the loss of that vibration which we had become accustomed to feeling as a natural part of our surroundings. It creates a void in our vibrational sensors.

For most of us that void doesn't feel good. We physically (and, of course, mentally, emotionally, and spiritually) miss the vibration of that individual. In general, most of us 'hurt' when that vibration is taken away from us. When someone close to us leaves us, we feel bad.

The question is, is feeling bad about the loss of a loved one a 'bad feeling' that we should try to move away from?

Personally, I don't think that trying to quickly move on to 'feeling good' will make us...feel good.

The truth is we have suffered a significant vibrational loss to our systems. And, it is virtually impossible that any new vibration that we can attract could replace that missing vibration in exactly the same way.

Old sayings endure through time because they have a large degree of truth to them. One old saying is that *"Time heals all wounds."* When it comes to losing the vibration of someone close to us, it takes time to fill that void with new and different vibrations. Since no new vibration is ever likely to fill that void in exactly the same way, there will always be a piece of that person's vibrations that we will miss for a long time, probably forever.

That is as it should be. I don't believe any of us want to forget someone we have known and loved. Just the thought of forgetting that person would, in itself, create a bad feeling in most of us.

Thus, the bad feeling we have when we experience the loss of someone close to us provides us with a contrast that allows us to feel how important that person was in our lives. A part of us <u>wants</u> to feel that loss and wants us to honor how fortunate we were to have had the chance to experience the vibrations that person emitted in our presence.

To honor the loss of that person and to experience the contrast of their missing vibration is useful to our well-being in the short-term. But, to dwell on it forever is not what life is about. Dying is only the end of the physical manifestation of a person's vibrations. The energy that manifested itself into physicality simply converts back to non-physical energy.

There is scientific validation of this concept. The First Law of Thermodynamics states that energy is neither created nor destroyed. Energy can change into different forms (mass and energy) but the energy within is neither created nor destroyed during the conversion. The amount of energy remains the same regardless of its form. When we convert from our physical energy form into a non-matter energy form, our energy doesn't disappear. It just takes on a different form, a different vibration.

It is not that the energy and vibrations of the person we loved have disappeared; it is more like those vibrations have changed to a different frequency, one that we are not tuned into as well as the old frequency. We cannot expect to tune into radio station 710 on the AM dial and expect to hear the music of the station transmitting at 1020 on the FM dial.

What does this have to do with the question of whether it is sometimes okay to have a bad feeling? The point is that feelings are <u>always</u> telling us something important about our lives.

In the simplest form, we might say that bad feelings tell us when we are not attracting the life we want, while good feelings tell us we are living a life that is giving us more of what we want. But, life is not about getting all that we want. <u>The purpose of life is to learn, explore and notice the contrast between what feels good and what feels bad, so that we can direct our lives toward what feels better.</u>

If asked, many people would say they wish things wouldn't change so much. Many people wish that life would stay the same, predictable and normal. But, is that really what we want?

There is a story about a man named John who died and found himself standing in front of some pearly gates. Another man was standing just behind the gates and this man came out to welcome John.

Man: "Hello, John. Welcome. We're sorry that you recently passed away, but we are happy to have you with us now."

John: "Yeah, well, I guess I'm glad to be here. I was never sure what would happen after I died. I guess I'm kind of glad to find out there is a 'hereafter' after all".

Man: "I have looked at your records and they show that you were a pretty decent sort of person during your physical life. Because of that, we want you to have a pleasant life here with us. Have you given any thought to what sort of life you would like to live here?"

John: "Well, no, not really. As I said, I wasn't sure there was going to be any life after death so I hadn't put much thought into what kind of life I would like it to be."

Man: "I understand. Well, now that you're here, were there any parts of your past life that you really enjoyed? We can duplicate any environment or situation here, so what did you like doing before?"

John: "I guess one thing I liked a lot was being able go to fly fishing for trout in a lovely mountain stream. That always seemed to bring me pleasure and relaxation. That seems like something I would enjoy doing here."

Man: *"That sounds just great. I think we can set you up with something that will suit that description very well. Follow me."*

John followed the man and soon found himself standing in a beautiful mountain park, with a lovely meadow, and a clear, cold trout stream. There beside the stream was his old fly rod, his fishing vest full of his favorite flies, and even his favorite fishing hat.

John went down and looked into the water and he saw a beautiful rainbow trout, actively feeding in the middle of the stream. Everything seemed just about perfect.

John: *"Well, this certainly is beautiful. I couldn't have asked for a more perfect setting. Thank you for providing me with this wonderful place to be."*

Man: *"You're most welcome. I have to go now and take care of other things, but I'll stop by later and see how you're doing."*

The man left and John began rigging his rod to start fishing. He got everything ready and stepped down to the stream. He soon spotted that big old trout still feeding, and he cast his fly to it. The fly no sooner hit the water than the trout came up and ate it. John set the hook, played the fish, and finally brought it in. It was a fine three-pound fish. He admired its beauty, unhooked the fly, and released the fish back into the water to let it grow even bigger.

John re-rigged his line and moved further up the stream. He had only gone a couple of steps before he saw another fine trout, almost a duplicate of the first, feeding out in the stream.

He positioned himself to the side of the fish and cast out his fly to let it drift down in front of the trout.

As soon as the fly hit the water, the trout lunged for it. John set the hook and soon brought in another beautiful three-pound trout. Again, he admired the strength and beauty of the fish, and then let it go.

As the day continued, John found fish, cast to them, caught them and released them. It wasn't until some time later that he realized that every time he saw a fish, he hooked it on the very first cast. And, it was always a beautiful, three-pound rainbow trout.

As the day wore on, John felt a little bored with having the same thing happen over and over again. It was about this time that the man returned to see how John was doing.

Man: *"Well, John, how has your day been going? Do you like this setting and the fishing?"*

John: *"Well, it is quite beautiful, and the fishing has been great. Perfect, actually. But, you know, it's almost too perfect. I catch a three-pound trout on every cast."*

Man: *"Well, isn't that what you wished for?"*

John: *"Yes, I guess it is, but somehow, something just doesn't seem right. It's gotten really boring catching the same exact fish over and over again. Frankly, this isn't exactly what I thought Heaven would be like."*

Man: *"Who said anything about this being Heaven?"*

There is an old proverb attributed to the Chinese that says: *"Be careful what you wish for."*

Part of the experience of living is to experience the contrasts that life presents. To be honest, if everything were always the same, life would get real boring, real fast. While it may seem that having bad feelings is not pleasant, the truth is, if we didn't have feelings to contrast and compare against to determine what feels good versus what feels bad, we would live very boring, un-exciting, stagnant lives.

That isn't what life is about. Some things happen in our lives because we want them. We want them because we believe they will make us feel good.

However, it seems reasonable that we may also attract things that allow us to be able to compare and contrast between what feels good and what doesn't. The truth is, we can only know that something feels good when we can contrast it against something that feels worse. Sweet only tastes good because we have bitter to compare it against.

So, when you have a bad feeling, don't run from it. Notice it. A bad feeling is an indicator that you are doing something that doesn't feel good. But, it is just an indicator, nothing more.

We have the ability to create the life we want, to think about what we want, and to align our energy and our vibrations in order to receive what we want to attract. Acknowledge, respect, and give thanks for those bad feelings that help us know what we want. Then, move your thoughts toward where you want to go and what you want to be.

Bad feelings impact our lives in a negative way when we continue to dwell on them. There is no need to focus on them for too long. Let them show you when you are not following your wants, and then replace them with thoughts of what you do want.

***

Life is simple when we keep our focus on what feels good and what we want. Don't complicate your life by holding on to bad feelings from the past. Think about and create the life you want to attract, and then let your feelings guide you along the way.

14
Feeling Good the Wrong Way

Unfortunately, because some of us may have trouble remembering what feeling good naturally feels like, some people have gone for an artificial way to feel good. Drugs, alcohol, food, extreme sports, and excessive sex are some of the ways that people try to feel good artificially. In certain instances, people become addicted to these artificial mood enhancers.

Please understand that when I talk about going for the good feelings, I am not talking about good feelings that are produced artificially. In truth, these are just short-term distractions that do nothing to help people attract more of what they really want.

How can you tell if you are using something as an artificial way to feel good? There are a couple of indicators to watch for. If you notice that these indicators are present, it is likely that the feel good feeling you are getting is artificial, and not the real thing.

The first indicator is that an artificially-produced good feeling doesn't last very long. It may last an hour or maybe a day. But once the effects of the artificial stimulant wear off, you end up feeling just as bad as before, maybe worse. Drugs and alcohol produce these temporary good feelings, but they do nothing to improve your base feelings in the future. You have to consume more drugs and alcohol to produce the next good feeling. In addition, when the 'high' wears off, you not only feel bad, you also feel guilty for having given in to your 'weaker self.'

Food can produce the same temporary effect. I believe this is why so many people are fatter than they would like to be. They use food as a comforting, 'good feeling' producer. Unfortunately, the feeling only lasts as long as the last meal. The next day, the person is still fatter than they would prefer, and they also have feelings of guilt for having given in to eating.

There is nothing simple about breaking addictions. We allow these addictions to develop as a way to feel good for a little while and, we do this even though the effect is temporary and can have long-term negative consequences.

It is not the purpose of this book to give you concrete ways to break any addictions you might have. It *is* my purpose, however, to bring to your attention that an addiction is the way your inner self communicates that it isn't getting what it really wants.

This is another example of how it can be difficult to know and feel what really 'feels' good to us, versus 'thinking' what our minds tell us feels good. <u>Drugs, alcohol and other addictions only produce temporary good feelings in the mind.</u> What most of us want is to feel good all over, in our minds, hearts, spirits, bodies, and souls.

If you think about it (which is what many of us do when we try to 'think' our way through life), addictions are just leftovers from the past. In truth, to give energy and focus to an addiction will never get us closer to what we really want. Even complaining about being addicted does nothing but attract more of the addiction. Too many people have become addicted and habituated to feeling bad. The only way to change this is to want something else, something better.

What is that? I think for most of us the first step is to relearn what feels good to our inner self and to put our energy and focus on those things.

So, here is my question to you about trying a different approach. If you have been a person who tends to dwell in and on the past, how's that working for you? Are you wallowing in the bad feelings of the past, perhaps tied down by an addiction that only provides you with temporary good 'mind' thoughts? If the latter is your answer, what do you have to lose by trying something different?

It's doubtful that trying something different will make you feel any worse. And, maybe, just maybe, there is a chance that it might actually make you feel a little better.

***

You deserve to feel good in your inner self. Learn to use your mind to refocus your energy, your vibrations and your actions on what you really want. Only then can you attract natural good feelings. Only then can you break from the past and aim yourself in the direction of a better feeling future.

15
Too Many Choices Can Make Us Unhappy

As I have mentioned before, keeping things simple is something I strive for. When I keep things simple, I experience more good feelings. Unfortunately, our consumer-driven culture plays tricks on me and I often feel bad right after I make a choice. Let me explain.

Research shows that the more choices we have, the less satisfied we are with our final choice. In a research experiment, people were given a choice of six different types of jam. After they made their selections, they were tested to see how well they liked their final choice. Then the test was repeated with a different group of people only this time they were asked to choose from among 24 different jams.

The results showed that the more jams people had to choose from, the less satisfied they were with their final choice. This finding runs counter to our generally held belief that, the more options we have, the more likely we are to get exactly what we want.

(For me, this situation brings to mind the Starbucks Coffee Company. I must admit that I am concerned about what kind of society we are becoming when it takes longer to describe my order than it takes to drink it.)

Why would more choices make us less happy with our final choice? Before I answer that, let me share with you how we humans tend to operate.

I read a report not too long ago about how people react to good things and bad things. For some reason, the human species is wired to be more negatively impacted by bad things, than positively impacted by good things. We put more emphasis on avoiding feeling bad, than we do toward the pursuit of feeling good.

One example of this is the way people react to the stock market. People were tested to determine how they felt when their stock went up by a $1,000, versus how they felt if their stock went down by $1,000. The results showed that people felt almost ten times worse about losing $1,000, than they felt good about gaining $1,000. Again, it's counterintuitive, but it's true.

For the average bad feeling, we place a value of -10 on it. For the average good feeling, we only place a value of +1 on it. Thus, in general, we have to have 10 times more good feelings to balance out one bad feeling. It is hard to know whether this emphasis on 'bad' is a natural part of our makeup, or a learned tendency. Regardless, it impacts a lot of people and how they view life.

With that information in mind, let me explain why having more choices causes us to be less satisfied with our final choice. (By the way, with regard to purchases, there is a name for this syndrome…'buyer's remorse'.)

Since we don't like negative results, we will generally do our damndest to avoid them. Unfortunately, the more options we have, the higher the likelihood is that we will make…the wrong choice. Here is how this happens.

When we pick one jam from among six flavors, our subconscious minds calculate the probability that we will pick the 'best' one. (Remember, our subconscious minds constantly process a vast amount of information based on the last set of instructions we gave them.)

Thus, when we pick one jam from among six options, we have a one in six chance of picking the 'best' option. We have approximately a 17% chance of making the best choice.

Let's see what happens when we have 24 choices. The odds of making the <u>best</u> choice out of 24 options are only 1 in 24. Thus, we have only a 4% chance of making the best choice out of 24 options. Our subconscious minds quickly determine that we are far more likely to end up with the best choice when we have only six options to pick from.

Do you remember when you were a kid and you went into a candy store? If you went to a store that had just a couple of kinds of candy, it didn't take long to make up your mind. However, if you went into a store with hundreds of jars full of candy, your mind probably went crazy trying to make a choice from among all the options. And, when you left with a friend, didn't you often end up feeling like the candy your friend got was a better choice?

Fast forward 20 or 30 years and there you are, standing in front of a wall of HDTV's. All sizes and shapes and brands and prices and warranties and styles and optional remotes and, and, and…The truth is, when you get home after blowing your mind away with all the choices, you will be less happy with your final choice than if the store had only a half dozen TV's to pick from.

Let me give you one more example of the impact of too many choices. Have you gone into the grocery store or drug store lately to buy a simple…toothbrush? May God help us. We have to choose between ten brands, six levels of firmness, angled or not angled, wide, narrow, short, long, with and without tongue scrapers, 12 types of bristles, manual, electric, and from among 75 colors. By the time I get through all those options I'll probably be wearing dentures! My subconscious informs me that I have a better chance of winning the lottery than of picking the right toothbrush.

What does this have to do with improving the quality of your life and using attraction to get what you want?

<u>**If you don't consciously decide what you want in life, the world becomes a place that offers unlimited choices. If you don't consciously think about what you want and relay a clear set of instructions to your subconscious, you are setting yourself up to be disappointed with what you get.**</u>

This brings me back to keeping things simple. Before you go to the electronics store to select a new TV (or any other choice in life), decide for yourself what options are important. What size would work best in your living room? What price range can you <u>happily</u> afford? Do you really need a lifetime warranty or is the standard five-year warranty sufficient?

How can you know when you have come up with the best set of options? Simple. Choose the one that <u>feels</u> best. If $1,000 is too much to pay based on your current budget, thinking about buying a $1,000 TV…won't feel good. If you think about putting a 50" screen on a 48" wall…it won't feel good.

Our Emotions & Feelings Departments understand and integrate those conscious choices into our feelings. If we pay attention to how we feel…not how we 'think' we will feel, but how we actually feel…we are far more likely to be satisfied with our final choice.

This seems pretty simple when thinking about buying a TV. But what about when we have to choose a new job, move to another city, find a mate, or cease associating with someone who doesn't make us feel good when we are around them?

Even in these situations, we can eliminate many irrelevant options. When we consider moving to a new city, do we want to live in a warm climate or a cold one? Picking just one option reduces the total number of potential cities by 50%.

Do we want to live in a big city or a small one? We narrowed our options by 50%. By knowing what we don't want, we can narrow down the choices and home in on what we do want. Thus, you can increase your level of satisfaction with the choices you make by reducing the number of options you consider.

***

Too many options can be almost as bad as not having any. When you narrow your choice down to just two options, your subconscious will calculate that you have a 50/50 chance of making the 'best' choice. In this complex world in which we live, that may be as good as it gets.

16
There Is No Such Thing as a Bad Decision

Have you ever looked back at a decision you made and said to yourself, *"Man, that was a really bad decision?"* If you have, I would like you to re-consider whether it was a bad decision or not. But first, I want to give you some guidelines on how to determine whether the decision was bad or not.

Let's say you are about to make an important decision. Perhaps you are considering a new job, a long-term relationship, investing in a new business or buying a home. In the process of making the decision, you have gathered as much information as time and resources allowed and you must now decide what to do.

Let's assume you decided to buy a house for what seems like a reasonable amount, say $250,000. You make the decision, buy the house, move in, and three days later, you find out the house was built on top of a toxic waste dump. Bummer.

"Man! Deciding to buy that house was a really bad decision!"

Actually, it was not a bad decision when you made it. It only became a bad decision in your mind <u>after</u> more information came to light, information that you didn't have when you made the original decision.

(Please note: I would concede that we can make 'stupid'

decisions. A stupid decision is one where we knew about the negative information <u>before</u> making the decision. Case in point, the decision to buy a house if you <u>knew</u> it was built on a toxic waste dump would qualify as a stupid decision in most people's minds).

But let's go back to the concept of a bad decision. Whenever we make a decision, no matter how large or small, at the time we make the decision we have a finite amount of information to factor into it. If based on the information we feel that it is a good decision, then it is.

If two seconds after we make the decision we get more information; and if that new information makes it look like the original decision will not give us the outcome we had expected, it still does not make the original decision a bad decision.

Why? Because you made the first decision based on the best information you had available at the time. The fact that you got new information later and that information changed the outcome of your first decision is irrelevant to the quality of the first decision. Had the new information not become available, the first decision would still have continued to look like a good decision ten days later or even ten years later.

"But now I'm stuck with a house built on a toxic waste dump," you say. *"It certainly doesn't feel like I made a good decision."*

Well, that is true for sure. You definitely don't feel good about owning a house that glows in the dark when the lights aren't on.

But, here is the point of this discussion. What is to be accomplished by feeling bad and feeling guilty and convincing yourself you made a bad decision? Nothing. Feeling like you made a bad decision will not make the toxic waste disappear.

Feeling guilty and stupid will not make you feel any better or attract a good resolution to the problem. In fact, it will only attract more…toxic waste!

So, what is to be done at this point to get back to feeling better and attracting what you do want in your life? Simple. Make a new decision based on the new information you now have at hand.

"But now I feel like I'm just likely to make another bad decision."

Well, if that is what you think, feel, and believe, you're right. If you believe you are likely to make a bad decision, that is exactly what you are likely to attract.

Let me reiterate this important point. <u>You didn't make a bad decision the first time</u>. If you had known the information about the toxic waste issue, obviously, you wouldn't have bought the house. But you didn't have that information.

You can't blame yourself for making a bad decision on information you didn't have. At the time you made your decision, it is just as possible that gold would later be discovered on the property. Same house, same decision, but totally different outcomes.

This issue of making what we believe are 'bad' decisions is even more unpleasant when it relates to people. While we might hope to know everything about another person before we make a serious commitment, this expectation is perhaps unrealistic in today's fast-changing world. Remember, we all come from dysfunctional families.

Early on in life, many people bury their natural frequencies and build walls to protect themselves from emotional and physical threats (or realities). They may spend many of their formative years (prior to reaching marrying age) trying to fit in, trying to conform to the way they thought the world wanted them to be.

Thus, when people get married, the person we marry may be very different at a core vibrational level than the person we see in front of us. As the marriage progresses, it may become more difficult for our spouse to hide and harness those previously buried feelings. Thus, we can potentially find ourselves married to a very different vibrational person than the one we thought we fell in love with.

Unfortunately, at that point, conflicts can arise, static can overwhelm the relationship, and it can be easy to come to the conclusion that getting married was a really **bad** decision. In truth, it wasn't a bad decision. We make the best decisions we can based on the information we have at the time. Thus, if getting married seemed to be a good decision based on the information at hand, it was. The fact that new information would present itself later and change the basis of the relationship could never have been foreseen or predicted.

We make hundreds of decisions every day. All we can do is to make those decisions based on the information we have available at the time. In essence, we simply do the best we can with the information we have. Then, if we get new information, we can make a new decision and put our beliefs, energies and vibrations to work in support of that new decision.

Can you see how believing in something (like bad decisions) can cause you to attract more of the things you don't want?

We would all like to make decisions that align perfectly with what we want and who we are. What we don't want is to waste time beating ourselves up or to feel guilty because we think we made a 'bad' decision. It was NOT a bad decision. The truth is, despite our best intentions and efforts, life sometimes takes a turn in ways that could not have been foreseen.

***

Don't waste time fretting over what you believe was a 'bad' decision. Wasting time feeling guilty about the past <u>never</u> gets us closer to what we want. Focus on moving forward by making a new decision based on the new information. Only by focusing on what we want can we attract it.

17
Will the Real 'Me' Please Stand Up?

The most common question I get asked when I meet a person for the first time is:

"Is Hawkeye your real name?"

I guess it depends on what the person means by the word 'real.' Hawkeye is not my given name, the name that appeared on my birth certificate. However, Hawkeye is my legal name. It is on my driver's license and my Social Security account. I legally changed my first name to Hawkeye about ten years ago. Why? No, it wasn't because a bunch of creditors were after me. I changed my name because I didn't vibrate well with the name my parents gave me at birth.

Now, I can hear you saying, *"Oh, that's just silly. What do you mean you didn't vibrate well with your name? Of course you did. It was your name. Why wouldn't you vibrate well with your own name?"*

My original name was the first name of a World War II Air Force pilot who was an Ace. (He shot down five enemy planes to be awarded the title 'Ace'.) My father was in the Air Force during the war and I guess he thought a lot of this man. Truthfully, I never understood why I was given the name.

Regardless, I never liked my name. Never related to it. It was never a name I felt good about. Of course, as a child and as a young adult, the thought of changing my name would never have entered my mind. It was...my name.

In 1994, after I sold a company I owned with two partners, I wanted to become a speaker. I liked speaking (still do) and wanted to give speeches and seminars on various aspects of business and life that I had learned during 25 years of consulting. It was at that time that the idea of changing my name occurred to me. I thought about it like an actor who decides to have a different 'stage' name. I discussed it with my wife and she felt that if I wanted to change my first name to something else, that would be fine, as long as the new name I selected wasn't 'Sue'!

At the time, my mother and father were still alive. When I raised the possibility of my name change with them, I got pretty much the response I expected: Dad didn't care at all, and Mom wasn't too thrilled with the idea. It was then that I realized something about my mom and dad that I had never really thought about until that moment.

My dad's real name was Irvin. But, my mom called him "Jim." When Mom asked me why I wanted to change my name, I asked her why she called Dad, Jim, instead of his real name. She said that she never pictured Dad as an "Irvin" and thought the name Jim suited him better. That was all the ammunition I needed to convince her that my name change was a good idea.

Of course, then I had to decide what I wanted my new name to be. My nickname was given to me by friends who called me Hawkeye because of my ability to see things, especially things in nature: elk at 1,000 yards on the other side of a mountain valley; four leaf clovers that I spotted on the ground while walking at a brisk pace; a trout dimpling the surface of the water as it fed along the edge of a stream. From that perspective, the name Hawkeye felt natural. It vibrated at my frequency.

During the 25 years I had been a marketing and management consultant and coach, I made a living spotting things that weren't right about how a business operated and how it marketed itself. Thus, the name Hawkeye related well to what I did for a living. I decided that Hawkeye was a name that felt good and fit who I was, so I legally changed my name.

Why am I including this story about changing my name in a book about getting your it together? Because it illustrates how something as simple as your name can impact how clearly you vibrate, even with yourself.

I was at a Christmas party a year ago at the home of a business owner who was a client of mine. This woman, whom I'll call Teresa, had a few friends and business acquaintances over to celebrate the holidays and she invited my wife and me to attend. At the party, Teresa introduced me to her husband, Jason. As often happens, Jason immediately asked me the usual question: *"Is Hawkeye your real name?"*

I gave my usual answer and a brief account of why I had decided to change my name.

Jason got very quiet. He looked like a person who had either been struck by a bolt of lightning, or had come to a major revelation about himself. When I asked him what he was thinking he said, *"I just realized that I don't like my name, either."*

He went on to say that Jason was actually his middle name. His first name was Eric. He said that as a child, he had always been called Eric. But, in high school, one of his friends started calling him Jason. Soon, everyone called him Jason, even his family. The name Jason stuck, and he just went along with it.

But, now, he realized that he didn't think of himself as Jason. He liked the name Eric. It had always felt good to him. It was who he was in his own mind. It vibrated at his frequency.

From that moment, Jason went back to using the name Eric. His wife was amazed that this man she had known only as Jason since the time she had met him and married him, felt so strongly about being called Eric. And yet, everyone who knows Eric could see, could sense, could feel, how much more comfortable he was with the name Eric. He had his business cards changed, changed his email address, and even got a new nameplate for his desk.

Six months later I ran into Eric and he thanked me for pointing out the importance of a name. He said it was like a weight had been taken off his shoulders, a weight that he never realized was there. His wife says that he is now a different person, but, in truth, he is the person she had been attracted to when they first met. He is Eric.

Please understand that I am not advocating that you, or anyone else, should change your name just because you are unhappy with certain aspects of your life. The point is that we are vibrational beings. When we work to eliminate the static that creates discord in our internal vibrations, little things can have significant impacts on us. With that in mind, let me mention other things that can create static in our vibrations and disrupt our lives.

What kind of clothes do you wear? What kind of clothes do you feel most comfortable wearing? Are you a person who likes to dress up even if you are just going to lounge around the house? Or are you a person who feels happy wearing blue jeans and a t-shirt? If you like to dress up, you probably don't want to get a job as a life guard at the beach. On the other hand, if you like to wear shorts and flip flops to work, you probably shouldn't become a lawyer.

These are extreme examples of clothes being inappropriate for specific jobs, but they are excellent examples of how something simple can create static. Think about it. We work at our jobs five days a week, and if our wardrobe is in conflict with our basic nature, it can be a constant source of static during 50% of our waking hours.

There are many other little things that can create static in our systems. My wife went to a women's party the other day. It was a party where they could get their nails done, feast on chocolate goodies, and just have fun. One of the things available was to get a 'makeup makeover'.

My wife does not wear a lot of makeup. Frankly, I don't think she needs to as she is pretty in her natural skin. And, she has never felt like she wanted to wear much makeup.

However, at the party, some of the women convinced her to let the makeup artist do her thing. When the makeover was complete, a number of women commented that the makeup looked good on her and that she should consider wearing it more often. My wife looked in the mirror and groaned. She didn't recognize the person in the mirror. As often happens in these situations, the makeup artist used products that she, the artist, liked on herself! Since my wife and the beautician do not vibrate at the same frequency, what was appropriate for one was all wrong for the other.

My wife said that while she appreciated the comments and the woman's effort, she just didn't feel good wearing makeup. The woman who applied the makeup then said: *"Oh, you'll get used to it. You just have to give yourself some time to adjust to the new look."*

Get used to it? Take time to adjust to the new look? Say what? The fact was that my wife didn't like the look, didn't feel good in that look, and was not the least bit interested in having to "get used to it." That look was not who she is anymore than wearing combat boots would be. When she got home, (and after seeing the look in my eyes which only confirmed her own feelings) she removed the makeup and went back to being the naturally beautiful person she has always been.

How many times do we allow ourselves to take on vibrations that don't harmonize well with who we naturally are? Too often, I'm afraid. It can be ordinary things like clothes or cosmetics or 'the look' we are told we should have that create ongoing static...static which keeps us from vibrating in a natural way that makes us feel good.

This concept can impact us in many areas of our lives. What kind of car do you drive? Assuming you can afford a choice, do you feel better driving a sedan or a pickup truck? Do you like the color blue or do you vibrate better with red? Do you like country western music but have to listen to 'talk radio' eight hours a day at work? That would be enough to mess up anyone's vibrations!

All I am suggesting is that you pay attention to how you feel. <u>If you notice that you feel out-of-sorts, antsy, stressed, tired, irritated, or depressed, pay attention to the environment around you.</u>

Let me give you another example of how your environment might impact your ability to reduce the static in your vibration. Feng shui (pronounced fehng-shway) is an ancient Chinese system that uses aesthetics to help improve a person's ability to receive positive Qi (pronounced 'chee', meaning energy). Modern believers in feng shui say that something as simple as the proper placement of objects (such as furniture) can help people achieve their goals and clear their vibrations.

Do you have a place in your home (or office) where you can go to calm your nerves, settle your thoughts, and clear some of the static out of your system? Most of us don't have time to climb a mountain to get our it together. Therefore, we need to create our own space where we can focus our thoughts, energies and vibrations on what we want in life. Maybe you would benefit from creating a space for yourself where you can go to get your it together.

I called this chapter *"Will the Real 'Me' Please Stand Up?"* because too often we seem to let the outside world tell us how we should vibrate. We get so busy operating in static-creating situations and environments, that it becomes very difficult for the 'real me' to get through. It is hard to let our natural vibrations attract the life we want if the noise around us drowns out our song.

***

Pay attention to what feels good in all areas of your life. Be conscious of your environment, the people around you, and even the name you go by. Try to create an environment that has as much vibrational alignment with your natural vibrations as you can. This will allow you to attract those things that vibrate in harmony with you, and to attract the life you want.

18
Dr. Jekyll or Mr. Hyde?

In the last chapter I talked about the trouble we can have in finding the real 'me' amidst the static that surrounds us. It is easy to be inundated by the vibrations of our environment and the people around us.

In this chapter I would like to talk about this issue from another perspective. That perspective is: What kind of a person are you?

We all came into the world with our own unique frequency. No two people vibrate exactly the same. However, we have certain vibrations that make us better suited for some things, and less well suited for others. Knowing what your vibrational tendencies are can help you find the work you enjoy, the place you want to be, and the people you want to be around. In essence, the better you know yourself, the more likely you will be able to attract the things in life that will vibrate in harmony with you.

There are many ways of categorizing people: race, religion, politics, geography, culture, ethnicity, height, weight, shoe size, hair color, and what kind of donuts you like to eat. All of these factors contribute to our vibrational makeup and, therefore, to what vibrations we find most attractive.

Another way to categorize people is based on their emotional, psychological, personality and behavioral tendencies. It is these tendencies that I would like to discuss for a moment.

Have you ever taken a personality test? There are lots of different tests which measure many different characteristics. Some of the more well-known tests would include the Jung-Myers-Briggs test, Enneagram, DISC, and others. What these tests are designed to do is to help you understand how you tend to operate and behave in life, both in your personal and business lives. Some are designed to help you find an occupation that matches well with your personality type. By knowing what your personality tendencies are, you can focus your intentions on attracting the types of careers, environments, and co-workers who are more likely to vibrate in harmony with you.

I like to keep things simple. The easiest way for me to categorize many of the basic vibrational tendencies of people is to determine how they vibrate in two particular categories. Those categories are:

- Introvert/Extrovert

- Task-oriented/People-oriented.

Think about two scales that would categorize you by these two different characteristics.

Introvert…1 2 3 4 5…Extrovert

Task-Oriented…1 2 3 4 5…People-Oriented.

If you think about people for a moment, do you like being around people, or are you more comfortable being by yourself? If you like being around lots of people, you are more of an extrovert. If you like being alone or around a few people, you are more of an introvert.

Another interesting way of categorizing Introverts and Extroverts was given by Marti Olsen Laney, Psy.D. in her book "*The Introvert Advantage*". To summarize, Laney offered the thought that Extroverts like to spend time <u>with</u> people to recharge their internal batteries. Introverts, on the other hand, usually need to spend time <u>alone</u> to recharge their batteries.

Contrary to what many people who know me might think, based on Laney's definition, I am an Introvert. After I attend a meeting or a party or an event where there are lots of people present, especially noisy events like conventions, sports, or entertainment functions, I have to go home, retreat to my cave, and give myself anywhere from a couple of hours to a day to recover. If the event is especially chaotic, it can take a couple of days before I get my vibrations back to normal.

When it comes to the category of task-oriented versus people-oriented, I tend to lean toward the task side. While my job frequently requires me to work with people, I prefer doing tasks with one person or a small group.

One of the 'personality' tests I took a couple years ago was called the DISC assessment. (If you would like to learn more about this test, you can go online to http://www.onlinediscprofile.com.) One of the interesting things about this particular test is that it gave two sets of readings about my basic nature. One set of readings described how I tend to operate in my work environment. The other described how I like to operate in the comfort of my own home.

On the work scale, I was high in the categories that would describe the basic prototype of a consultant. Big surprise there. I have been functioning as some kind of consultant for the last 30 years. Apparently I had learned pretty well how to vibrate like a consultant.

More interesting, however, was the fact that I do not prefer to operate as a consultant in my personal life. In essence, my work persona and my home life persona were two significantly different people. I'm a regular Dr. Jekyll and Mr. Hyde!

As a coach/consultant I need to operate pretty well on the extrovert side of the scale. However, in my natural state of being, I prefer to be much more of an introvert. When I discovered this difference, I realized why I would often come home from a big convention with my vibrational systems all out of whack.

So, what does this have to do with <u>you</u> getting <u>your</u> it together and attracting the life you want? Plenty.

If you are an extrovert and people-oriented, getting a job as a lookout in a forestry fire-spotting tower would probably drive you loony. On the other hand, if you are an introvert and prefer to work on tasks instead of with people, being the primary organizer of a major NASCAR race is probably not a good career choice.

If we plan to get our it together, we'd better know what our basic tendencies are and what keeps us vibrating in harmony with ourselves. Without that knowledge, we can't focus our intentions and attract the life we want.

Too many times I see people trying to be someone they are not. Too many times I see people struggling in an environment that vibrates in opposition to their basic nature. Too many times people believe they should imitate successful people. This throws them out of their natural rhythm, and into chaos.

What type of person are you? I don't want you to think about the type of person you <u>think</u> you have to be because of the job or situation you are in. I want you to try to feel in your vibrations the person you feel best being.

How can we ever expect to attract the things we want in life if we burden ourselves with situations where we have to pretend to be somebody else? We can't. Attraction responds to the vibrations you emit. If you are pretending to be a significantly different type of vibrational person than is your natural state, you will attract more of the vibrational chaos you emit. Whatever destination you are trying to reach in your life, if you vibrate like the chaos of Las Vegas, you are unlikely to get to the soothing beaches of Tahiti.

Now would be a good time to stop and think about what kind of vibrational being you are. What makes you feel good? Lots of people? Working alone? Typing on a computer in the quiet of your home? Playing team sports in loud stadiums? You can't expect to attract solitude if you constantly tell your Subconscious Processing Department that loud noise, busy streets, and hoards of people are your default operating instructions.

***

If you are having trouble determining what your natural tendencies are, perhaps taking one of the tests I mentioned will give you a start toward understanding the types of jobs, places, environments, and the number of people that best suit your vibrational nature. Then, once you have a better understanding of what your basic vibrational nature is, it is up to you to focus your intentions, energies and vibrations toward attracting that kind of life.

19
I Can't See the Forest for the...Me's?

Have you ever noticed how easy it is to see when other people are not vibrating in harmony with themselves? As vibrational beings, we are both senders and receivers of vibrations. For some reason, it's easy to sense the vibration of others when they are burdened with static. But why, then, is it often so difficult to recognize the static in ourselves?

As a business consultant and coach for much of my career, I have long known that it is difficult for a business owner/manager to look at his/her own business objectively. We get so involved in the business, so close to the day-to-day problems and operations, that we can no longer see some of the problems (and solutions) that are often staring us right in the face. This is the essence of the old saying: *"I can't see the forest for the trees."*

I believe that a similar problem exists when we try to look at ourselves from the inside. Between losing touch with our natural vibrations and being inundated with the static vibrations of those around us, it is often difficult to *'separate our forests from our me's'*.

There's no doubt about it, we are complicated beings. Can you imagine how confusing it must have been for that first human to think *"I am"*? Wow! What a mind blower! And then, s/he was faced with an even bigger problem: Who could s/he talk to about it? Bummer.

A case can be made that we need other people with whom we can interact to be able to define who we are. When we try to talk to ourselves, the conversation is pretty one-sided. When we try to evaluate ourselves from our internal vacuums, we end up either with a lot of empty space, or with too many conflicting opinions. In either case, we have difficulty trying to determine who we are and how well we are doing when we look at our lives from our internal point of view.

In truth, we all compare ourselves to others. We do this to understand who we are, who we aren't, and perhaps, who we want to be. Understand, however, that there is a difference between comparing and judging.

Comparing simply lets us see how we are the same or different than others. In comparing ourselves to others, we try to figure out which vibrations feel good and which vibrations are not in harmony with our frequencies. Comparing helps us determine how and when we vibrate most harmoniously in our lives.

Judging, on the other hand, means that one way of vibrating is better than another. The bad news is that judging never gets us closer to knowing what we want or any closer to getting what we want.

One way that we can focus on what we want and keep our systems more static free is to allow someone to be a sounding board for us. The definition of a sounding board is:

"a person whose reactions serve as a measure of the acceptability of an idea or course of action."

Notice the definition does not say that a sounding board is someone who judges the appropriateness of an idea or course of action. They merely give us their reactions to our thoughts and actions and we use their feedback to help us fine-tune our own vibrations. A person who serves as a sounding board can help us see when we are vibrating in harmony with our wants, or in serious conflict with our natural tone.

Being a sounding board is the role taken on by coaches, counselors, priests, ministers, gurus, psychologists and psychiatrists. We look to these people to provide us with an outside, unbiased perspective of how we are doing. In the best cases, these people put aside their own issues to help others define their wants and direct their thoughts, energies and vibrations to be in harmony with those wants.

Can a family member, a friend, or perhaps a coworker take on the role of an unbiased sounding board? That is a tough question to answer. Most of us have our own issues that we are working on. (Remember, we <u>all</u> came from dysfunctional families!) Because of that, it may be a good idea to seek out a person who is not in constant contact with the vibrational sources of our static, someone other than family members, close friends, or associates.

Also understand that <u>it is not the role of a sounding board to tell us what they think we should do</u>. Their role is to ask us questions that will help us define our wants, and to provide support in helping us maintain our focus as we pursue those wants. A person who serves the role of sounding board is like an external part of our Subconscious Processing Department. They can help us filter out the noise and stay in tune, but they cannot decide which songs we want to play.

How do we know if we could use a little help to clarify and pursue our wants? A number of indicators might lead us to believe that we could use a little assistance.

- If we have trouble defining what we want, sometimes another person can ask questions that will free our minds from having to be both the questioner, and the responder.

- The other person is also more likely to ask us the tough questions that we would not ask ourselves (because we are uncomfortable having to think about them).

- After we have defined our wants, our sounding boards provide the support to feel better about ourselves and the motivation to fulfill our wants.

Getting our it together is not necessarily an easy process. It is all too easy to slip into old habits and find ourselves once again dwelling in the past. Our sounding boards help us keep our focus on where we are headed. And, on occasion, our sounding boards provide us with a good, swift kick in the pants to get us off our <u>but's,</u> and back to moving forward on our <u>and's</u>.

Successful CEOs, professional athletes, actors and actresses, politicians and entrepreneurs believe in the value of having sounding boards to help them stay focused. If it helps these people stay focused, why not you and me?

***

If you have trouble defining your wants and keeping your focus directed toward what you want to attract, consider talking to someone who can help you jump start your journey and help you achieve your goals.

20
I Want to Be Like Mike

I talked to a woman the other day who said she had practiced the concepts of attraction for a number of years. While she felt that she had benefited from focusing on her wants, she wasn't getting the results she wanted. She asked me to review her approach, especially as it related to her work.

Jackie was an independent representative for a national firm that motivated its reps and helped them meet their personal goals. The company frequently offered training programs on positive thinking and personal development. The programs were designed to help reps get their it together and achieve their potential.

One of the things she heard at these trainings was the importance of having a role model. She mentioned how many times Napoleon Hill's great book *"Think and Grow Rich"* was referenced. She had especially taken note of the discussions about the benefits of having a Mastermind group to assist us in achieving our goals. Jackie wanted to identify someone who was successful and then model herself after that person.

Jackie chose Sheila as her model. Sheila was a very successful saleswoman in the company. Sheila had been one of the top ten reps in the company for five years running, and was in the top twenty salespeople of all time.

Sheila was an outgoing, high-energy, Type A personality who set her goals and then worked with a tenaciousness that guaranteed her success. She was single, 40 years old, and had never been married. Her career had always been her top priority.

Jackie watched and listened to everything Sheila said and did. She spent as much time as possible around Sheila at company meetings, conventions, and presentations. Jackie believed that if she could just take on some of Sheila's 'success vibrations', she, too, would be successful.

Jackie had tried to be like Sheila for the previous two years. Unfortunately, she never came close to the level of success that Sheila enjoyed. In fact, after a couple of years, Jackie realized that her sales had actually gone down from what she had been doing two years earlier. She wasn't getting closer to what she wanted; she was getting farther and farther away.

As I listened to Jackie tell her story, I took a moment to notice the person sitting in front of me. Jackie was in her late thirties and was married with two children. She had worked for awhile before she got married and had her children, but had only re-entered the work force after her youngest child started school. She had chosen to be an independent sales rep because it gave her the freedom to work on her own schedule and be around when her children came home from school.

Jackie was smart, attractive, and focused on what she wanted. As she sat in front of me, she spoke quietly, used subtle hand gestures, and smiled a wonderful, natural, gentle smile.

As we visited at a local Starbucks, a prospect Jackie had cultivated for over a month walked in and ordered coffee. When Jackie saw this person, she asked if I would excuse her for a moment as she wanted to go say hello to her prospective customer.

As Jackie stood, she mutated before my eyes. She became effusive, spoke in a much louder voice, and gestured wildly as she talked. She pounced on the poor woman, shook her hand harder and longer than necessary, and proclaimed how glad she was to see her.

I cringed as I watched this display. Jackie had become... Sheila!

Jackie had not only watched and studied how Sheila behaved, she had done her best to vibrate the same way Sheila did. Jackie was trying to be a Type A personality like Sheila. She tried to exude confidence, look powerful, and grasp this prospect in her Sheila-like clutches.

Unfortunately for Jackie, this attempt to vibrate like Sheila was, to put it mildly, a total disaster. Instead of coming across like a confident Sheila, she came across like a pushy, obnoxious sales person who was about to pick the meat off the bones of her intended prey. The woman grabbed her latte and fled, no doubt happy to escape with her life.

When Jackie sat back down, she was breathing fast, sweating a little, and still talking loud and fast. It took the better part of five minutes before she changed back into the person I knew.

It was evident, at least from my perspective, why Jackie was not successful in her work. She thought the only way she could become successful like Sheila was to become Sheila's clone. Jackie did not understand the secret of Sheila's success.

What is Sheila's secret? Is it because she is a Type A personality? Did she come from a wealthy family? Does she mimic the behavior of someone else? What is the secret behind the successful people in the world?

The secret to success is to be yourself. The secret to success is to decide what you want, and to focus your own thoughts, energies and unique vibrations to attract what you want. The secret is to decide what you like to do, to enjoy your work, and to attract other people, including customers, who will love you for being the static-free person that resides at the heart of who you are.

If you think about successful people, you will find a huge variety: men, women, old, young, married, single, divorced, white, black, Asian, American, Spanish, Scottish, Protestant, Catholic, Islamic, republican, democrat, independent, bald, ugly, pretty, smart, dumb, loud, quiet, humble, egotistical and…successful.

Therefore, success is not determined by some set of looks, genes, upbringing, belief system, or culture. Success is not attained when we become someone else. Success occurs when we focus on our own wants, when we are in tune with our own natural desires and frequencies, and when we attract the kind of people who vibrate in harmony with our natural selves.

Successful people don't let other people disrupt their harmonious vibrations with interference and static. Successful people don't use other people's definition of success. Successful people don't spend time comparing themselves to others. They go after what they want, often with a single-minded focus, and they don't give up until they have achieved it.

When books tell you to look to successful people for advise or direction, don't look at who they are, how they act, how they talk, or how they dress. Don't try to become that person.

- Look at how focused they are.

- Listen to how articulate and passionate they are about what they want.

- See how consistent and persistent they are.

- Watch them shrug off the occasional setback and look for new and better ways to move ahead.

There's an old story about Thomas Edison and his view of success and failure. Apparently, Edison failed to create the light bulb more than 1,000 times. He put it this way, *"I have not failed 1,000 times. I have successfully discovered 1,000 ways to NOT make a light bulb."*

The point is, even if you try and fail, it doesn't mean that you didn't learn something. Successful people don't waste time worrying about failure. They stay focused and know they will find the answer.

Successful people don't think about having to work hard. When they work, they think about the result, not the task. They might work 14 hours a day without a thought about how much time they put in. Many successful people wish they had 30 hours in a day so they could spend more time doing what they enjoy.

If you think about successful people, you see these traits regardless of the type of business they are in. Donald Trump loves financing and building things. Michael Jordan loves basketball. Oprah loves acting and interacting with people. Whether they are in sports, entertainment, politics, science, religion, education, retailing, manufacturing, or finance, successful people love what they do. And, because they love what they do, they have an enormous amount of energy to focus on getting what they want.

There is one more thing that successful people do. They seldom lose sight of doing what <u>feels</u> good to them. That doesn't mean they always feel good. They do, however, have an intention to move past what feels bad, and to move toward what feels good. In essence, they vibrate with the universe. They vibrate in harmony with their own conscious and subconscious minds to attract what they want into their lives. And that is what they do attract.

If you have trouble attracting the success you desire, it is fine to watch successful people to understand how they vibrate to achieve what they want. But, don't try to vibrate at the same frequency they do. Learn to vibrate in your own frequency and direct your energy toward what you like to do, and toward what makes you feel good.

***

Success is not measured by how much money you have. The real measure of success is how good you feel while living your life.

21
I've Got the Pedal to the Metal...
But My Parking Brake's On!

The title of this chapter sounds like great lyrics for a country western song, don't you think? Unfortunately, I meet a lot of people for whom these words would describe their lives.

In previous chapters I talked about how difficult it is to attract what we want when we are in conflict with our natural vibrations. In Chapter 20, I talked about Jackie and how she tried to be a clone of Sheila. Unfortunately, Sheila was an extrovert, while Jackie was an introvert. Thus, whenever Jackie tried to vibrate like Sheila, she had the pedal to the metal (Sheila vibrations) but her parking brake was on (Jackie vibrations).

The result? Jackie ended up going nowhere fast.

There are times when I, too, suffer from this condition. The words I use to describe my feelings are: *"I'm getting in my own way"*. We all do this now and again. We have good intentions, but we lack clarity about what we want and how to attract what we want. We end up running hard...but going nowhere. Unfortunately, this situation leads some people to have even worse feelings about themselves. They end up believing they are failures.

A woman I coach brought this subject up during a recent conversation. Carla (not her real name) was depressed because she had been working hard for many years to attain certain goals she had set for herself. But, after more than ten years of hard work and dedication, she found herself no closer to her goals than when she started.

She admitted that she had enjoyed a pretty good life during those years. She made a decent salary, had a good husband, took occasional trips, and owned a nice home. Nevertheless, she had not achieved a couple of her important goals.

She expressed her great sadness when she said: *"My life is just one big disappointment. I'm a failure."*

Regardless of the life a person has led, no one should ever have to look back on life and think they failed.

When I thought about her words later, two things came to mind. First, I realized that she was a failure in <u>her</u> mind because she compared her accomplishments to some arbitrary standard society set as the definition of success. She even mentioned the name of the person she had used as her role model.

Unfortunately, unbeknownst to Carla, the person she had chosen as her role model had inherited all of his wealth. Born with the proverbial 'silver spoon in his mouth', he had never done a real day's work in his life, and there was nothing about his 'success' that he had achieved himself. Nevertheless, Carla believed that he was successful and that she wasn't, despite all her hard work. Thus, she was a 'failure'.

Secondly I realized that Carla had unintentionally set herself up for this 'failure'. Outside influences had played a large role in setting her up for what she considered to be her eventual failure.

Much like Jackie, Carla tried to vibrate like the successful person she took as her model. Unfortunately for Carla, her model also happened to be a man. Carla tried to act the part of a successful businessman. She dressed only in suits. She kept her hair trimmed short. She didn't wear much makeup and she belonged to business groups comprised mostly of men.

Unfortunately, Carla's natural vibration was the opposite of the vibration of her chosen model. Before she embarked on her quest for success, Carla had loved to write, to sit by the seashore, and to enjoy quiet dinners with friends and family. She came from a big family that accepted her for being the wonderful, unique person she was.

All that changed when Carla decided that the only way to be a 'success' was to go out and make a name for herself. She left her home town, went to a big city, got a job at a large company, and began her pursuit of success.

Now, ten years later, she felt like a total failure. She never reached that pinnacle of success that she had built in her mind…an unattainable vision based on false assumptions, mistaken ideas, and standards that would not have brought her happiness even if she had attained them.

Carla had the pedal to the metal in her pursuit of success. But, because her natural internal vibrations were tuned to a totally different frequency, she was doomed to run hard and go nowhere. Her internal parking brake was set hard and fast to keep her safe in a place where she was in harmony with herself and the people around her.

I see and talk to a lot of people who find themselves locked in this conflict, torn between being the person they think they <u>are supposed to be</u>, and being the person they really <u>are</u> in their hearts. It is a prescription for failure.

I met with Carla a week later and shared some of my thoughts with her. She cried when she realized she had put herself on a quest for something that she didn't really want. It comforted her to learn that it had not been a lack of effort or desire or skill that had kept her from achieving her misguided goals.

In truth, part of her, the part that protected her inner well-being, had done everything it could to keep her from pursuing the false standards of success. Those standards would never have been enough because they didn't fit the 'real' Carla. The real Carla fought from the inside in a desperate attempt to focus her thoughts, actions and vibrations on the things that would bring her true happiness.

I felt good that Carla could now refocus her intention on those things she knew in her heart that she wanted. I felt good right up to the point when, with a tear running down her cheek, she looked me in the eye and said: *"I have been a total failure at listening to my heart."*

I tried to think of something to say that might cheer her up, but, it would have been pointless to say anything. This was a pain that would take some time to heal. Nothing I could say was going to change the last ten years…lost years as far as she was concerned.

I told her that it was all right to take some time to grieve, but I wanted to see her again to help her begin to focus on the rest of her life. I felt confident that her life could still bring her real happiness, the kind of happiness and satisfaction she would know and feel in her heart.

Carla was not a failure. The truth is she never had a chance at success in the way the world defines it. And, even if she had achieved those false goals, she still wouldn't have been happy.

There are many people in the world who are labeled 'successful' by external standards. Unfortunately, many of them will never feel successful by their own standards. At some point, they will feel guilty because they will believe they have been total failures at listening to their hearts. That's a bitter pill for anyone to swallow.

What are your goals? What kind of life do you want to live and attract? Is it a life based on a set of standards that ignores the heart and only feeds the ego? Or is it a life based on the wants of the heart? Determine what success means to you and what feels good in your heart. Otherwise, you are setting yourself up to look back from a future time and judge yourself to be a failure.

**

How can you know if you are pursuing your real wants? Pretend that you have achieved your goals and notice how that feels. Successes of the ego are felt in the mind. Successes of the heart are felt…in the heart.

22
Allowing the Good to Come Into Your Life

Why is it so hard to change the way we think and act when we know in our hearts that those changes would give us a more productive, worthwhile, and meaningful life? I believe one of the reasons we resist change is because throughout our lives, we have built walls around us to protect us from being hurt. We built these walls to keep from being mentally, emotionally, and even physically hurt by the world and the people around us.

Building walls seems to be a natural human trait. We all do it. We start building our walls at an early age and we both maintain and reinforce those walls as we go through life. We build new walls as we deem necessary, and we build these walls for one specific reason...to survive.

Some people say that building walls around ourselves is a bad thing. I disagree. As children, we do not have enough life experience to confront our fears with a conscious, direct response. At the same time, our survival instinct, one of the most powerful instincts in human beings, causes us to take whatever steps are necessary to protect ourselves from the threats we perceive. These threats can be real...like being beaten by an abusive parent...or they may only be imagined threats...like thinking *"I'm not pretty enough so nobody will ever love me."*

The good news is that our walls do their jobs very well. In most cases, we survive. But surviving is not the same as living. <u>Surviving</u> is hoping that by making it through until tomorrow, things might get better.

<u>Living</u>, on the other hand, is enjoying the present for what it is, and looking forward to the new and exciting prospects that tomorrow offers.

The bad news about walls is, once we have built them, once we see that they have allowed us to survive (a point totally reinforced by the fact we are alive to have the thought), we conclude it is in our best interest to keep those walls up forever.

We keep walls up and often reinforce them even though the original threat no longer exists. Why? We keep walls up because we were hurt the first time when we didn't have a wall up to protect ourselves. And, we're not about to let that happen again, are we? Even though we know that the original threat is long gone, the part of us that looks out for our survival says:

"Hey, stupid. You can't tear that wall down. What if the threat reappears? If you tear that wall down, we may not have time to get it built back up again when the old threat comes back!"

This is a very powerful argument we have with ourselves. It is an argument that we may acknowledge at a conscious level, or it may reside deep within our subconscious. Regardless, the worse the original hurt was, the more important we believe it is to keep that wall up for future protection.

While it may be true that *"time heals all wounds,"* the passage of time alone does not erode our walls. Even when the original pain is a faded memory, our walls stand tall and strong, ever vigilant for the threats of the past.

Unfortunately, once the original threat is gone, our walls become fortresses that we think will keep us safe inside. But, in truth, they can become more like prisons, never letting us escape from the past.

> **Walls not only keep the bad out,**
> **they also keep the <u>good</u> good out.**
> **The walls <u>we built</u> keep us locked inside.**

Not only do our walls keep the 'bad' out, our walls keep <u>everything</u> out. When that big, strong, impenetrable wall surrounds us, NOTHING can get in.

> **Even goodness cannot get in.**

This is very important so let me repeat it. When our old walls surround us, the good cannot get in either.

I wish that this was the total extent of the problem. Unfortunately, there is another negative effect that our walls have on our lives in addition to keeping the good from getting in:

> **Our walls keep <u>us</u> from getting out,**
> **and they keep us from throwing the old,**
> **'bad' past away.**

Behind our walls, we never get to see the beautiful sunrises and sunsets. We can't see the children playing out in the field. There are wonderful things to do and see and taste and feel outside our walls, but we never get to experience them when we are trapped behind the walls of the past.

Even when someone offers to come inside our walls to visit or to bring us a lovely gift, we can't seem to let them in. And so, the world that has so many good things in it simply passes us by.

A little melodramatic you say? Maybe. But it is my belief that we all keep walls up; different kinds of walls. And, it is hard to break down those walls. It is hard to leave the perceived 'safety' of our prison even though we may be unhappy, unproductive, and unsatisfied living a life of the past.

It is likely that our walls will always be a part of us. In fact, we can accept and honor how well our walls have protected us over the years. However, those same walls hold us in one place and prevent us from reaching our destination and fulfilling our wants. They keep the good out and prevent us from experiencing all the joy and beauty that exist in the world.

In order to live a full life we must think about and decide what we want, put our energy, thoughts and vibrations behind our desires, and then…allow the wonderful things we attract to come into our lives.

For many of us, our good thoughts and desires attract the life we want. But, even the power of our attraction can't break through the old walls of the past. <u>We can attract the life we want, but we have to be open enough to let it in.</u> We have to trust that we are strong enough to venture out from behind our walls and to receive the goodness that we seek.

We also have to be willing to throw away the 'bad' from the past and move forward in search of the goodness that we want to attract. Otherwise:

**If we insist on dwelling in the past,
we will find ourselves still living there in the future.**

***

Now is the time to venture out from behind your walls. Think about what you want. Put your desires and vibrations and actions behind what you want, and be open to letting in the happiness, health and prosperity that you can attract into your life.

23
You Are a Perfect Attractor

The other day a friend told me she couldn't seem to attract what she wanted. The harder she tried to attract what she wanted, the less she got.

I asked her how she phrased her wants. She said things like: *"I want to attract what I want. I am focused on attracting a better job. I am working hard to attract a person with whom I can have a meaningful relationship."*

While these might seem to be reasonable phrases to attract what we want, a problem arises when we focus on the act or <u>process</u> of 'attraction', instead of focusing on <u>what</u> we want to attract.

For some people, even the word 'attract' has negative vibrations. For some, the word 'attract' is related to a 'lack of having'. Focusing on the word 'attract' causes some people to emit a vibration of 'lack'.

Attraction is automatic. We cannot turn it on, nor can we turn it off. We attract what we have told our conscious and subconscious minds we want. But, if we haven't given ourselves clear instructions, or if we allow things to come by default, we will attract more of the lack of clarity we vibrate.

Let me repeat this. We attract what we vibrate, either by intention or by default. This is automatic and it happens every minute of every day. We do not want to focus on the <u>act</u> of attraction. We simply want to focus on <u>what</u> we want to attract.

The woman I mentioned earlier was focused on the <u>act</u> of attracting. Her thoughts were along the lines of: *"I need to think about attracting what I want. I'm not spending enough time attracting what I want. I didn't do a very good job of attracting what I wanted today."*

In truth, she couldn't do a better job at attracting because she (and all of us) are attracting at full power every minute of every day. However, when we don't attract what we want, we can get confused and start thinking that we are doing a 'bad job of attracting'. <u>We can never do a bad job of attracting. We can only do a poor job of focusing on what we want to attract.</u>

This is an area where different words may help us create the vibrations of what we want to attract, instead of focusing on the act of attraction. Here are some ways this woman rephrased her words to get her vibrations in harmony with her wants.

"I am making good progress toward finding a job that I will enjoy and one I can do with like-minded people I will enjoy working with."

"My thoughts, my energies, my beliefs, and my vibrations are clearly focused on allowing into my life a warm, loving, friendly, happy person with whom I can share my dreams."

"I feel good when I think about having enough money to do the things that I enjoy."

"I can imagine how good it is going to feel when I am living a healthier life and eating more nutritious foods."

These statements help us focus on <u>what</u> we want to attract, not on the process of attracting.

***

Remember, the process of attracting is constant and automatic. Our only job is to make sure that our words, our thoughts, our beliefs and our actions create vibrations that are in harmony with what makes us feel good. Try to write statements and describe what you want without using the word 'attract'. When you are clear on <u>what</u> you want to attract, the process of attraction will take care of itself.

24
Celebrating Our Successes

One of the reasons we may not enjoy the full benefits of what we attract into our lives is that we forget to stop and celebrate our progress, our achievements, and our successes. Too often we focus on what we didn't get done, and forget to enjoy what we have accomplished.

I know people who make detailed lists of the things they want to do. They get to work, look at their lists, add new things, adjust priorities, and then they dive into their work to see how many of the things they can accomplish in a day. And that is good.

At the end of the day, however, they look at the list, quickly check off the things they completed, add new things that came up during the day, and then set their sights on what they will tackle tomorrow. And that's where the problem lies. These people start and end their day thinking about the things that still need to be done, not what they actually did.

If we are to believe that attraction brings to us those things we focus our thoughts, energies and vibrations on, what will we attract if we always start and finish our day thinking about what didn't get done and feeling like the list will never end?

A list of our wants and the things we want to accomplish can help us stay focused. However, if we always focus on what <u>hasn't</u> been completed, we will attract an endless list of things that still need to be done.

If we think about what we want to attract as a journey, too often, at the end of the day we ask ourselves the standard question that kids ask on a trip: *"Are we there yet?"* And, of course, unless we have accomplished our ultimate objective, the answer is always *"No."*

Generally speaking, *"No"* is not a word that generates good feelings in us. *"No"* focuses on the fact that we haven't gotten where we want go. *"No"* doesn't give us any feeling of satisfaction for how far we have progressed on the journey.

Having a list of things we want to accomplish is like taking a trip. Too often, we start out the day with a big list, we make progress and get some things done, but at the end of the day, when we ask ourselves if we completed the list, the answer is usually *"No."* Even if we have completed nine tasks out of ten, we still focus on the one that didn't get done. Bummer. With this approach, we end up suffering through another never-ending day at work that will be followed by yet another never-ending list of things to do tomorrow.

Is it any wonder that we feel unfulfilled in our work? At least at the end of a real road trip, we usually get to play or rest a bit once we reach our destination.

If we always focus on what we haven't gotten done, that is what attraction will bring to us…more things that haven't been done. So, I would like to suggest a simple little change to help us enjoy our accomplishments, celebrate our successes, and attract more of what we want into our lives.

At the start of the day, let's look at our lists, add things that need to be added, adjust the priorities, and put our full energies into our work. But, at the end of the day let's draw a line through the things we <u>didn't</u> get done. Then, let's stop and take great pleasure and satisfaction in all the progress we made and all the things we did accomplish.

This same concept applies to our lives outside of work. When we have our written list of the things we want to attract into our lives, some of them may be attracted in a day, others may take years. If all we focus on is the fact that we don't have them yet, we will probably never get them.

On the other hand, when we focus on the progress we make toward fulfilling our desires, we can focus our thoughts, energies and vibrations on how good it will feel when we complete that portion of our journey.

If we want attraction to work for us, we need to focus on how far we have come in our progress toward our wants, not on the fact we aren't there yet.

***

Don't focus on how far you still have to go. Focus on how much closer you are to reaching your goal. Focus your conscious and subconscious minds on the road ahead and the progress you have made. Acknowledge and celebrate your successes and more success will come to you.

25
Opportunity Just Knocked. Were You Listening?

Some people believe that the concept of attraction works because it attracts those things on which they focus their thoughts. They believe they don't need to work towards what they want. In fact, some people believe if they work toward what they want, they won't get it.

I think there is a mistaken belief (actually, there are probably many, but we'll just deal with this one here) about how attraction works in our lives. Let me see if I can offer some guidance and explain what it means to work for what you want.

There is nothing wrong with working toward what you want in life. Furthermore, working toward what you want will not prevent you from getting it if what you are working on…is what you want. The only way that working will get in the way of getting you what you want is if you are working on…what you don't want.

Think about it. People who love what they do are pretty good at getting their it together and fulfilling their desires. Why? The vibrations of their work are consistent with what they want to attract. Unfortunately, too many people have unfulfilling jobs they don't like. When they don't define what they do want, they struggle and end up doing something that brings them no joy and no pleasure. They try hard to do something which never gets them closer to what they really want.

Now, a few of you may be thinking:

"I think I have done a pretty good job of deciding what I want. I also feel that I am doing a pretty good job of focusing my thoughts and attentions and actions towards attracting what I want.

"However, it doesn't feel like I am making much progress. Am I doing something wrong or have I just not given things enough time to work?"

It is quite possible that you do a fine job of focusing your attention on what you want. The question is, if opportunity knocked on your door, would you hear it?

There is an old saying that "opportunity knocks but once." Unfortunately, because we often have not done a good job of focusing on our wants in the past, we may not realize it when we are attracting what we wanted.

There is a story about a preacher who had his ministry in a small town in the South. One year the area around his parish received a huge amount of rain over a couple of days and some major flooding occurred (no, not over 40 days…it wasn't that flood!)

Many people's homes flooded, and many people were at risk of drowning. The church was on higher ground so the minister was safe. But, wanting to serve his community, he struck out in one of the rescue boats to see if he could help save some of the other people who were trapped on the roofs of their homes.

It wasn't long before the small boat he was in was full of people. Unfortunately, there were still many people who needed to be rescued. So, the minister helped the people on one roof into the boat and then he climbed out onto the roof himself. He told the man driving the boat to rescue the other people still trapped on adjoining houses, and that he would be fine until the man could come back and get him.

Later in the day as the rain continued to fall, the man in the rescue boat came back to get the minister. But, the minister could still see many people trapped on other houses, so he told the man to make more trips and then to come back for him. Three different times the man came back but the minister continued to direct him to rescue the others instead.

Unfortunately, darkness came quickly and on the final trip, the man driving the rescue boat couldn't find his way back to the minister. The next day, when he finally found his way back to the place where the minister had stayed, he discovered that the house had been washed away. The minister's drowned body was found a few days later after the flood had subsided.

The minister, upon meeting his demise, soon found himself at the gates of Heaven, and there to meet him was St. Peter.

St. Peter: *"Hello, Minister Jones. Glad to have you with us. How are you doing?""*

Minister: *"Well, I guess I'm doing all right, but I'm a little surprised that I drowned in the flood. I thought I had served God pretty well in my ministry on earth. I'm a little surprised He let me die while I was helping my parishioners."*

St. Peter: *"Well, Minister, to be real honest, we're a little surprised to see you here, too. We sent three boats to rescue you. Why didn't you get in one of them?"*

Sometimes we are so busy we fail to notice the arrival of the very thing we want to attract.

Attraction <u>will</u> bring you what you want to attract (or what you vibrate to attract by default). However, it will not slap you upside the head to tell you that what you wanted has arrived at your doorstep.

Some of us may also fail to realize that what we attract may not look exactly like what we expected. Suppose you want to attract $1,000,000. You might think that it will show itself by winning the lottery. In reality, it may come to you when someone offers you the opportunity to invest $10,000 in a little startup company called Microsoft.

The more detailed you can make your wants, the easier it may be to recognize when you have attracted what you want. But, don't get so specific that you aren't open to having your wants satisfied in new and perhaps even more satisfying ways.

Attraction responds to the <u>vibrations</u> of what you want, <u>not the exact blueprint</u> you may have in your mind. If we focus too much on the detail of the blueprint, we may fail to notice the beautiful opportunity that is presenting itself right next to us.

***

As you focus your attention on your wants, don't get so tied-up in the details that you fail to notice what you <u>are</u> attracting into your life. It would be a shame if your ship finally came in, but you were too busy to notice its arrival.

26
Big Boys Don't Cry

As I read through the chapters of this book, I realized that many of the people I used as examples were women. They are based on real people, with the names changed to protect their identities. I intended no bias or innuendo when I used so many stories about women.

The truth is, I meet and talk about these subjects with more women than men. Why? Because big boys don't cry.

It is just as difficult for men to decide what they want, and how to attract what they want, as it is for women. However, even though there was a movement afoot in the '80's for men to 'get in touch with their softer and gentler sides', most men still believe that the right way for a 'real' man to act is to be tough, strong, and masculine. No Beanie Babies allowed.

Thus, most men don't feel free enough or comfortable enough to talk about life issues, even to other men. Or maybe especially to other men. Women, on the other hand, have always talked with other women about such issues. And, many women talk to men about such topics if the man is a good listener.

Men and women <u>are</u> different. John Gray covered many of these differences in his 1992 book: *"Men Are from Mars, Women Are from Venus"*. Men and women have different ways of communicating. Women like to sit and talk to other women. They like to share their stories, needs and concerns. But, they do not always ask for solutions.

Men, on the other hand, have evolved to believe that it is our duty to solve problems...any problems...all problems. Thus, when a woman shares a problem with a man, he assumes that, in order to fulfill his duty as a man, he must solve that problem.

In many instances, the woman doesn't want someone else to solve the problem. She only wants someone to listen (like her women friends would) as she talks about how she might deal with a particular issue. Unfortunately, because of the basic difference in the way men and women approach issues, lots of vibrational static can be created when Venus just wants to communicate, and Mars feels the need to solve the problem.

Please understand that this is not a book about male/female relationships. My only purpose in raising this issue about men is that, for many men, it isn't any fun believing that we always have to be strong and to hide our frustrations and feelings. Too often, when men try to 'keep a lid' on their feelings, the pressure eventually builds too high and we explode in a fury of anger and emotion.

Yes, I have been there and done that; not proud of it; try not to do it very often. But, the truth is, we men are just as susceptible to being inundated by the static of the world as women. We, also, are 'only human', we just don't like to admit it.

The point I want to make in this chapter is that, in any place you find a woman's name being used in a story in this book, you could just as easily put a man's name, too. Life is a challenge for all of us. We all have to work at getting our it together.

***

GETTING YOUR 'IT' TOGETHER

It doesn't matter whether you are a man, a woman, a guru, a doctor, a beach bum, a TV repairman, a secretary, a weatherman, or, heaven forbid, a politician. Getting and keeping our it together is a life-long process. The only thing we must decide is whether we will unconsciously let the world dictate the life we will have, or that we will consciously focus on attracting the life we want.

27
No News Is Good News

Do you watch or read the news each day? If so, how does it make you feel? Maybe it's just me but, I have a hard time finding anything in the news to feel good about.

At the time I am writing this book the news stories include: politics, war, famine, tsunamis, crooked business people, bad weather, murders, accidents, shootings, drug busts, recession and the crashing stock market. Of course, the truth is, if I had written this a year ago, 50 years ago, or even 1,000 years ago, the names might have changed, but the topics would have been the same.

Most news is not good news. This is the origin of the statement "No news is good news." Generally, if there aren't many substantive stories in the news, not a lot of bad things happened that day.

As if reporting only bad news is not enough, it appears that the worse the news is, the more time and resources are allocated to report it. The bigger the disaster, the more airtime and printed pages that are assigned to overwhelm us with every gory detail.

When we decide to focus on our wants, and to use our beliefs, energies and vibrations to attract those wants, how often do you think the news will help you achieve your desires? Do the vibrations you pick up from the news make you feel better than you did before you watched the news?

Please understand that I'm not telling you to stop watching the news. I will suggest, however, that if you don't feel good when you watch the news, don't do it.

"But," you say, *"I need to watch the news to stay abreast of what is happening in the world. Something important might happen that I need to know about. Besides, if everyone else is talking about a hot topic in the news, I don't want to appear stupid by not being up-to-date on what is going on."*

Those sound like good arguments in defense of watching the news. But, I think there is a chance that watching the news is just one more habit that we drag along with us, a habit that really doesn't make our lives feel one bit better.

Too often, when we hear about or read bad news, we immediately feel bad. And that is as it should be. Feeling bad tells us that something in the world disturbed our natural vibration and it doesn't feel good to us. It tells us that something isn't in harmony with our wants.

However, once we register that bad feeling and become informed about what happened, we have a tendency to get stuck in the bad news. Continuing to discuss, debate, read about, or watch the ongoing (or should we say…never-ending) reports about a disaster or tragedy does nothing to improve the situation or make us feel better.

When a tornado wipes out a town in Kansas and a dozen people die, we should feel bad when we hear the news. However, once we register how bad we feel, the best thing we can do for ourselves and those who were impacted is to…decide what we want to do and then move forward.

If you decide you want to go to Kansas and help the tornado victims, then go. If you decide that you want to donate goods or food or money to those who lost their homes, then do so. Think about what you want to do that would be in harmony with your wants and your vibration.

<u>Focus on what you want in your life and put your thoughts, energy and vibrations behind making that happen. If you continue to dwell on something bad, you achieve nothing positive…either for yourself, or the people affected by the tragedy.</u>

This careful assessment also applies to the television programs we watch, the movies we go to, the books we read, and the events we attend.

I'm fascinated and dismayed by the latest trend in TV shows…the reality show. Reality? Whose reality? Not my reality. Frankly, it amazes me that so many people like to watch other people being stupid, degrading, mean and petty, and that was just on *"Dancing with the Stars."*

And don't get me started on soap operas. When I was growing up, soap operas like *"The Edge of Night"* were only on during the day. Now, they are thinly disguised as dramas in hospitals, businesses, police stations, casinos and any other place directors can conjure up to air all of civilization's dirty laundry.

I don't know about you but I don't look forward to watching a show that portrays nothing but the worst that humanity has to offer: cheating spouses, paranoid relatives, divorces, abortions, terminal illness, lying business partners. I think some people watch soap operas just so they can convince themselves that their own lives, as bad as they seem to be, are at least better than the lives of the characters in the show.

Do we really feel better when we watch people treat each other like crap? When we watch these shows and feel all the negative vibrations emitted, do we attract good things into our lives? Sorry, but I just don't think so.

As I more consciously decide the things to which I will give my attention, I also decided that I want to attend movies that make me feel better coming out than when I went in. That doesn't mean that all the movies I watch are rated PG. However, I will be honest and say that I prefer to watch movies with happy endings. Watching another movie about war, sex, violence, marital failure, drugs, or 'How to Screw Your Buddy' doesn't make me feel good. And, I have <u>NO</u> desire to attract those things into my life.

There are a few movies I watch over and over again. They are probably not on many people's Top Ten list, but, for me, they portray characters who decided to go for what they want, no matter what.

Movies that I find uplifting are: *"Down Periscope"* with Kelsey Grammar, *"What Dreams May Come"* with Robin Williams, *"Groundhog Day"* with Bill Murray, and *"Bicentennial Man"*, also with Robin Williams. All of these movies portray characters that struggle with the way their lives are going.

These movies all portray characters who decide that the way their lives are going is unacceptable. They put all their energies and thoughts and actions into going after what they want, and Heaven help anyone who gets in their way.

In *"Bicentennial Man"*, Robin Williams portrays an android robot that gets dropped on his head and becomes sentient. He spends the rest of the movie trying to become a real human being, one who just happens to be contained inside a mechanical body. At a number of points in the movie, Robin is confronted with situations that he finds unacceptable. The line that he uses that best expresses his will to go after what he wants is simple: *"That will never do."*

Once he has made up his mind on what he wants, he focuses all of his intention and actions to get exactly what he wants. In some cases, this takes years. Ultimately, it takes a lifetime…a two-hundred year lifetime before he finally gets what he wants.

Bill Murray in *"Groundhog Day"* lives the same day over and over again. He eventually concentrates on living in the now, the present moment. With each successive day, he learns new things, helps others and enjoys doing the simple things. It is at that point that his life begins again with a new, and finally, different day.

Kelsey Grammar's character in *"Down Periscope"* is a classic 'Misfit Makes Good' story. Kelsey is challenged when he has to try to restrain his brilliant, happy-go-lucky personality as he operates in a strict, military setting. This often brings disastrous results (ramming a Soviet submarine and getting a poorly-located tattoo). But, through it all, he still manages to stay true to his inner frequency expressed so eloquently in the statement: *"God I love this job!"*

In *"What Dreams May Come"*, Robin Williams' character is presented with perhaps the worst nightmare a person might endure. Robin's wife is stricken with guilt over the loss of their children who died in a car accident, an accident for which she blames herself. When Robin dies, his wife can no longer bear the grief alone and she commits suicide. Because of this, she is doomed to spend eternity in a place worse than Hell.

Upon his arrival in Heaven, Robin finds out about his wife's situation from his son and daughter, plus a couple of other helpful souls. But, just like in *"Bicentennial Man"*, Robin's character takes a basic stance on this situation which is *"That will never do."* He proceeds with his full intention to save his wife, regardless of the risk to himself.

As for you ladies who are reading this, there are, of course, also great female characters who confront many of the same issues. Some movies that come to mind include *"Contact"* with Jody Foster; *"Legally Blond"* with Reese Witherspoon; and *"Chocolate"* with Juliette Binoche.

What do all of these movies have in common despite their different plots and stories? All the main characters are regular people, confronted with the same fears and guilt and troubles that many of us experience. They are not special.

Most of them believe and feel that they 'don't fit in' with the world around them. And for the most part, they are not happy living lives that aren't exactly what they want.

Yet, each of these characters finally trusts his/her heart and goes after what they want with little concern for the consequences. They pursue what they want with a focused intention and end up attracting the outcome they desire.

They discover that the way they 'fit in' to the world, and the way they get more of what they want, is to just be themselves, not someone the world thought they should be.

These characters are good role models. Not as a newscaster or a submarine captain or a robot, but role models who symbolize what we can achieve if we focus our intentions to attract, act on, and receive what we want.

Let me make one final point about the discussion in this chapter. All of the things you watch, read, discuss, hear, feel and think help create and attract the kind of life you want. But, attraction will also bring to you all the negative things you don't want if you continue to give those things your attention.

<u>The more consistent you are in focusing on the things you do want, the more likely you will be to attract them.</u>

If you feel good when you watch the news, do it. If you feel good when you read a good mystery novel, do it. If you keep your frequency free of static when you watch an interesting movie, do it.

However, if you watch a disaster movie or read a horror novel or watch people beat each other to a pulp and it doesn't make you feel good, then stop watching that stuff.

***

Tell your subconscious what is really important by focusing on the good things you want to attract. Otherwise, if you persist in watching and hearing and reading about negative stuff that makes you feel bad, that is what you will attract into your life.

28
Black Holes Suck

Of all the strange and wonderful things that exist in the physical Universe, my favorite has to be Black Holes. When I come back in my next life, I think I want to be one. Talk about having the power to attract!

Think about it. A black hole can have the mass of a billion of our suns crammed into an area no bigger than the radius of earth's orbit. Astro-physicists speculate that at least one black hole sits at the center of every galaxy, and there are billions of galaxies. Through gravity, a black hole can attract and hold onto stars that are 100,000 light years away.

Yeah, okay, swell, you are saying. So what? I have raised this concept of black holes because I find them useful metaphors for attracting what I want into my life.

At the moment, you probably don't consider yourself to be a very big black hole. In fact, currently, you probably suck at being a black hole. But, that's good! Why? Because, until you consciously decide what you want in life and what you want to attract, you'd suck in even more stuff you don't want.

Reckless, unfocused sucking can attract all kinds of unpleasant things: Comets (ice-cold bosses); meteors (hot, flaming romances that flare up and then flame out on contact); asteroids (relatives who are dumber than bricks); entire solar systems (obnoxious neighbors and their kids). Frankly, you should consider yourself lucky that you currently don't have the ability to suck stuff from any farther away than the local grocery store.

But, all of that is going to change. Now that you have started to decide what you want, you might as well focus on sucking in only the things you really want.

Picture yourself as a black hole. You are going to attract what you want not through gravity, but through the 'magnetic-like' vibrations you emit. And, whereas a real black hole sucks in anything that gets too close, you have the ability to suck in only what you want and what vibrates in harmony with you.

Since you aren't a very powerful black hole yet, when you focus on the thoughts, feelings and intentions of what you want, you will only be able to pull in little things: A few extra bucks here and there, a friendly smile, a new friend.

But, remember, as a black hole, the more you suck in what you want, the more powerful your sucking power becomes. As you grow in clarity of thought, your vibrational reach will extend outward farther and farther. Soon, you'll be powerful enough to pull in anything within the city limits. (If you live in a farm area, be sure you never think about manure.)

Can you begin to feel how to attract good things into your life? As you venture out into the world, notice the things you <u>want</u> to suck into your life.

"Wow, I'd really like to suck that new car into my garage."

"Oh, man, I can hardly wait to attract that hot looking guy/girl into my life."

"I love the thought of pulling a bigger salary into my pocket."

Suck, suck, suck. Ain't it glorious? And, when somebody

tells you that their life sucks, you can turn to them and say, "*Yeah, isn't it great! Mine, too!*"

All right. Now that I have your proto-black hole attention, time to quit kidding around. If you think that your life sucks in a bad way, the reason is that you simply haven't done a good job of deciding what to suck in.

Sucking is not bad. <u>Undirected</u> sucking is bad. Reckless, unconscious sucking is bringing you all that garbage you don't want. And, unfortunately, you have become pretty powerful at sucking in what you don't want. In fact, you're sucking in stuff from clear across the country, and too often, you've been thinking about manure.

It's time to use the black hole that is you to suck in the things you want. It's time to suck in the job you want, the salary you want, the love of your life. From now on, when someone asks you how you are doing, tell them proudly that your life sucks big-time. Tell them you have so many good things coming into your life that you may have to turn down the sucking power until you can make room for it all.

When you start using this simple metaphor of being a black hole, here is what will happen. First, right after you tell someone your life sucks big-time, you will smile. And, believe me, nothing starts attracting good stuff into your life like a good smile.

Next, you're likely to laugh, and laughs have <u>major</u> black hole sucking power. Finally, the person you are talking to will either laugh, too (which means you just successfully attracted a good vibrational compatriot) or they will think you're crazy and will run away as fast as their feet will carry them (which means you just successfully dispelled someone you didn't want to be around!)

***

Whether or not you find the concept of thinking of yourself as a black hole useful, I guarantee you this. You <u>will</u> attract a lot more of the good things you want by picturing yourself as a powerful black hole, than by walking around being an unconscious donut hole.

29
Suffocated by an 800 lb. Gorilla

Do you sometimes wake up in the morning feeling like you have an 800 pound gorilla sitting on your chest? Have you woken some mornings and said to yourself, *"Man, I feel miserable!"?* We all have.

Sometimes it is physical pain from too much exercise, bad food, or a bout of the flu. Sometimes this weighed-down feeling is mental anguish caused by a deteriorating relationship with a significant other, stressful times at work, or too many bills and not enough money to pay them.

We can also suffer from the 'chronic' pain of believing we are unlikely to ever have the life we really want.

Regardless of the cause, we all experience times when we feel miserable, depressed, or, in the worst cases…defeated. But, believe it or not, that's okay. Feeling miserable <u>is</u> a feeling. Feeling miserable tells us that we are not focused on what we want.

If we feel like someone ran over us with a truck, it's time we recognize that our unique vibrations and frequencies are overloaded with damaging static. Those miserable feelings are red flags waved at our hearts, minds and souls telling us to pay attention, and to get our 'it' together.

There is another feeling I would like to mention. While it may seem an odd feeling to address (and may, for some people, even seem inappropriate to discuss), it is, nevertheless, a feeling that presents a useful metaphor to help us understand why we may be burdened with certain negative feelings.

The feeling that comes to mind is the feeling of being constipated. Most people know how uncomfortable that is. Unfortunately, some of our current, miserable feelings may be caused by holding on too tightly to old, miserable feelings. We sometimes allow ourselves to be constipated by the negative vibrations of past.

I want you to recognize that even basic physical feelings like being constipated are just indicators that we aren't focused on what we want. Feelings are messengers telling us to pay attention to what we are doing.

Many of us have been filling our lives with a lot of useless garbage. We have attracted rubbish like an unconscious black hole, sucking in a lot of negative stuff that we don't want. Even worse, we sucked in more trash than we were able to process through our mental, physical, spiritual and emotional systems.

The fact is, a lot of our systems are backed-up. Stopped-up. Plugged-up. We are holding on so tightly to all of that garbage from the past that even if we wanted to suck in some new, good stuff, <u>there is no place for it to go</u>.

I realize this discussion may be a little more graphic than you wanted to think about. But, if you want to feel better, you may have to release some of the residue of the past before you will be able to take in a new and better feeling future.

So, when you find yourself feeling miserable, simply say to yourself:

"Hey, I'm noticing that I feel really rotten. I've gotta get going. I need to get my 'it' together and push all that old junk out so I can make room for the new life I want to attract."

***

GETTING YOUR 'IT' TOGETHER

Sometimes the simplest way to start feeling better is to get the 800 pound, gorilla-of-the-past off your chest.

30
Some Days I Feel Like I'm Fighting a Losing Battle

Yesterday was one of <u>those</u> days. You know the kind. The alarm clock didn't go off and I had to rush to get to a meeting. Traffic was backed up to Saturn. All the dishes were dirty and there was no milk in the fridge.

The Internet link was on the fritz and I couldn't get my emails, especially the one telling me that the meeting I drove 40 minutes to get to, and ended up being late for...had been cancelled. The stock market went down another 500 points and my favorite hockey team lost in the final four seconds of the game.

I wrote a couple thousand words for one of the chapters of this book, and forgot to hit the save button before a power surge restarted my computer. However, I did receive 537 junk emails with no problems at all.

The little door that covers the gas tank of my car broke a hinge and now it flaps around like a mother bird pretending to have a broken wing. I have to take the car in, let them look at it, set an appointment to go back, leave the car again so that they can determine exactly what part is needed and get it ordered, and then take the car back yet another day to get it installed.

The price of a gallon of gasoline went up yesterday to a level that now costs more than I paid for my car. My health insurance rate went up so much that I get sick thinking about it. Too bad my policy doesn't cover mental health problems.

It also rained yesterday. One of the two days a year that it does that here in Tucson. The day after I got my car washed.

I forgot to get toothpaste at the store the day before yesterday and had to dig around in the wastebasket to retrieve the old tube to try to squeeze just one more squirt out of it... for the third day in a row.

Yes, yesterday was a <u>swell</u> day.

Frankly, on days when I seem to be pulling in garbage from most of the nearby galaxy, it's hard to believe I can attract the life I want. Where did I go wrong? Which 'blast-from-the-past' program did I accidentally tell my Subconscious Processing Department to run that caused my black hole to suck in all that negative stuff?

Do you ever have those kind of days? The truth is, we all do.

Fortunately, today is another day (hopefully not like yesterday.) Today I get the chance to refocus my attention on what I want with the hope that yesterday was just an aberration due to severe sunspot activity.

Regardless of why I attracted all that stuff yesterday, no amount of re-hashing it will change anything. In addition, when I stop and think about yesterday, I should congratulate myself on the fact that there was a whole lot more crap I could have attracted...but didn't.

I didn't get another infected root canal in one of my teeth (after having had five of them, believe we when I tell you that they are not on my most wanted list.)

I wasn't in an accident. I didn't fire myself at work. I didn't get sucked up by a tornado and spit out into Kansas.

The water heater didn't blow up; the toilet didn't get stopped up; and, even though I ate all those cheese blintzes at the restaurant, neither did I.

Maybe yesterday wasn't such a bad day after all. I mean, it really could have been a lot worse. None of those things that happened were life threatening. I woke up on the right side of the grass. I woke up in a warm place where I didn't have to shovel snow this morning. I had a good night's sleep with a roof over my head and my beautiful wife sleeping next to me.

My Subconscious Processing Department kept me from falling off the bed all night and there <u>was</u> one more squirt of toothpaste in the tube.

We all have those days now and again where it seems like we must be in some parallel Universe where we don't vibrationally fit it. Some of the stuff that happens can be very traumatic and sad. Some of it can be merely irritating and frustrating. But, in truth, even on our bad days, there are usually some things we can be grateful for.

When you have one of those less-than-perfect days, about the best you can do is to look for the good stuff, try to refocus your vibrations on the things you attracted that you did want, and then set your intentions to move forward toward the life you want. Complaining about yesterday will never make tomorrow better.

***

The next time you have a bad day, notice the bad feelings; say "Thank you" to them for reminding you that the things you attracted were not exactly what you wanted; and then climb back into the saddle and move forward. If you let yourself go backwards, you'll just end up riding through a lot of old cosmic dust.

31
Efficiency Experts

Do you have time to read this chapter? I know how busy you are. Never enough time to do all the things that need to be done. Not enough time. Short of time. Out of time.

We should have plenty of time with all the time-saving devices that technology has brought us: vacuum cleaners, dishwashers, microwave ovens, electric toothbrushes, high-speed Internet. What, exactly, are we doing with all that extra time we are supposed to be saving? And when we use all those devices to save time, where are we supposed to put that saved time so that we can retrieve it later and use it when we need it?

Beats me. I never stumble across any extra time in an old shirt pocket, in my wallet, or in any of my drawers or file cabinets. I never find any time stored in the safe or on a computer disc. I think that maybe this whole idea of saving time is just a Madison Avenue advertising gimmick to make us think we are going to end up with more time.

If we can't put time away into a 'time certificate' at the local bank, just exactly how are we going to find more time to decide what our wants are? How are we going to find the time to do things that will get us what we want?

Since we can't save time for future use, we may need to think of more efficient ways to use the time we have. For that, we should take a moment to study…trout.

Yes, I know. You're probably saying to yourself that I have spent too much time out in the hot sun of Tucson. What in the world could trout possibly have to do with learning how to use our time better?

One of my favorite ways to get my it together is to fish for trout in clear mountain streams. Because of that, I have spent quite a bit of time watching how trout behave. Trout lead pretty simple lives: they hatch; try to find enough food to survive; try not to be something else's food; and try to find another trout during spawning season to start the process all over again. It's the circle of life in the river.

Over the years, trout have learned how to use their energy wisely. For example, much of the food that a trout feeds on passes by in the middle of the stream. While some food exists in the quiet backwaters, the biggest part of the food buffet is out in the main current. Unfortunately, for a trout to feed out in the main part of the stream, it has to burn a lot of energy fighting the current.

Trout have learned to obtain more calories from the food they eat while out in the main, stream flow, than the calories they burn fighting the current. They are willing to burn extra energy gathering food when it is plentiful; but, when food is scarce, they rest and conserve their energy.

Pretty smart, don't you think? Seems like a darn good plan. In fact, trout are so smart that they have been instrumental in providing ideas and terminology to the business world. You didn't know that, did you? Well, it's true. For example, where exactly did you think the business world got the term "Ef-fish-iency Experts?"

So, the question is, how do trout and efficiency experts play a role in you getting your it together and attracting the life you want?

We all get the same 24 hours in a day. You can't buy extra time, save time in a bottle, or bide your time waiting for life to make you rich. Whatever you want in life, whatever you want to do in life, you get 24 hours each day in which to do it. Unfortunately, once a moment, an hour, or a day has passed, you will never have the chance to use that time again to improve your life. You can never save time to use on a rainy day.

As human beings, our lives are more complicated than a trout's. In addition to eating and sex, most of us have to work for a living. Many of us know the feeling of fighting against the current (as discussed in Chapter 8). In fact, many of us know how tiring it can be simply trying to find enough time to get the laundry done.

Therefore, our best hope for having more time may be through finding ways to be more efficient at doing the things we do. If we can learn to be more efficient, we might end up with some time left over to actually have a life.

One of the tools I use to be more efficient is the 80/20 Rule. This is not a new idea. The original concept was discovered by an Italian economist by the name of Vilfredo Pareto back in the late 1800's. But, like many simple ideas that have proven to be true, the 80/20 rule has not only survived, it has even been the basis of sophisticated business concepts like Total Quality Management and Six Sigma.

If you are not familiar with the 80/20 rule, here is the basic idea. In many things in life, we find that a very small percentage of one factor can be responsible for a much larger percentage of a related factor. Let me give you a simple example.

If you go into your closet and look at all your clothes, you are likely to find that you wear 20% of your clothes 80% of the time. In this example, a small percentage of the clothes you own accounts for a much larger percentage of the clothes you actually wear. The same holds true for the shoes you wear.

Of all the restaurants you frequent in your city or town, chances are you go to just 20% of them 80% of the time. In addition, of all the items on the menu at one of your favorite restaurants, it is very likely that you order about 20% of the menu items 80% of the times you eat there.

Will the numbers always be 20% and 80%? No, that's not the way the rule works. The 80/20 rule is simply the name we give to the way in which a small amount of one thing seems to have such a large impact on something else.

Thus, in truth, you might find that you wear 20% of your clothes 69% of the time. Or you might determine that of all the shows you watch on TV, you watch 20% of the shows 87% of the time. It is not the exact numbers that are important. It is important only to note how one factor can account for, or have such a significant impact upon, another.

So, what does the 80/20 Rule have to do with making us more efficient at attracting the life we want? If you stop and analyze the people you know, you are likely to find that approximately 20% of the people you know account for 80% of the good vibrations you get from all people.

Think about that for a moment. Let's say you know 10 people. Let's assume that you spend one hour with each of them during a week. If you think about which of those people are most harmonious with your unique vibration, you are likely to find that just two of those ten people provide you with 80% of your 'good-feeling-people-time'.

Regardless of what the exact numbers are, you will find that a small number of people provide you with a very large percentage of the good feelings you receive in your interactions with people overall.

What this also means, however, is that you may be spending 80% of your time with people who only give you 20% of your 'people pleasure time'. If this is true, how does that feel? How do you feel about spending 80% of your time with people with whom you don't vibrate well? Probably not very good.

The question is, wouldn't you rather spend 80% of your time with the 20% of the people who give you 80% of your enjoyment? Any changes or choices that you can make that will allow you to have more time with your harmonious 'friends' would be...time well spent, don't you think?

"But, Hawkeye, I don't have much control over who I have to spend a lot of my time with."

Maybe that is true. Maybe you can't easily reallocate your time to be able to spend it with people you like. But, that is only true of the present. What about in the future? What are you doing to focus your intentions, your beliefs, your energies and your vibrations to be able to spend more time in the future with people with whom you vibrate well?

The concept of the 80/20 Rule can be applied to virtually any aspect of both your personal and your business lives. Do you currently spend only 20% of your life on things that give you 80% of your good feelings. How would it feel if you were able to spend 80% of your time doing things that make you feel good?

Let me give you one more simple example of how we can use concepts like the 80/20 rule to help us improve the quality of our lives.

Do you like pie or cake? What is your favorite kind: cheesecake, chocolate cake with chocolate icing, carrot cake, pecan pie with whip cream, strawberry shortcake? Think about the best piece of pie or cake you ever had.

Now, think about how good the first bite was. Just thinking about it makes your mouth water, doesn't it? Rich, creamy, decadent even. Then, you take another bite that's almost as good as the first. However, by the fourth or fifth bite, each successive bite is not nearly as glorious as that first bite. By the time you have eaten most of it, you are primarily just trying to clean your plate.

If there are 20 bites in a piece of cake, it is likely that you will receive 80% of the overall pleasure of eating it in the first four bites (four is 20% of twenty). After those first four bites, the level of gratification from each successive bite goes down. Often, we eat the last few bites even though the pleasure we receive from them has gone down to virtually nothing. Why is that important?

Are you a little overweight like I am? I certainly seem capable of attracting a great piece of cake into my life. And, on too many occasions, I eat the whole piece without thinking about it. Unfortunately, by eating the whole thing, I also attract extra calories that I would have been better off without.

Did I get a lot of extra pleasure out of eating the whole piece? No, not really. And I felt guilty because I ate the whole thing and am a little heavier than I care to be. Thus, some of the good feelings I received from eating that first glorious bite were lost because I didn't keep in mind that I also want to feel good in other aspects of my life.

When I look back on that piece of cake, I realize that I could have quit eating after the first four bites and ended up feeling a lot better overall. In the first four bites I experienced most of the pleasure of the taste of the cake. By eating the rest, I didn't increase my good feelings related to taste, and I negatively impacted my feelings related to my weight.

You might find it useful in the future to think of the 80/20 Rule in relation to things you buy, things you eat, things you do, people you spend time with, and places you go. Doing anything in excess can add more bad feelings to our lives than good feelings.

As I discussed in Chapter 3, living life from a perspective of always wanting 'more' seldom brings us much satisfaction. When you think about what you want to attract into your life, remember to make conscious decisions about how much would be <u>enough</u> to satisfy your desires. When we tell our conscious and subconscious minds that we would love to have a piece of cheesecake, it would also be useful to remind ourselves that the first four bites would be more than enough to satisfy our desires.

How will this help you have more time to focus on your wants and to have the life you want? Why, just think of what you could do with the time you would have otherwise spent eating those last sixteen bites.

***

If you want more time to have the life you want, learn to become an ef-fish-ciency expert like the trout. Learn to save your time, your energy, and your vibrational resources for the things you really want in life.

32
Dead Batteries

I have recently given thought to coming back in my next life as a hybrid vehicle. I like the idea of being able to recharge my batteries by plugging myself into an electrical socket. Come home at night; park myself in the garage; plug myself in; and wake up with a fresh charge the next day. Sounds nice and simple, doesn't it?

As I get older, it gets harder to get a full charge on the old set of batteries that is 'me'. Maybe I should come back as the Energizer Bunny. That way I could just keep going and going and going.

The question I have for you is, what do you do to recharge your batteries when they get run down? Do you take time off occasionally to put a full charge on your system, or do you have to jumpstart yourself every morning just to make it out of bed?

Did you know that the average American worker takes fewer days of vacation than workers in any of the other developed countries in the world? Sad, but true. Yes, we are a nation of workaholics. What is hard to understand is why businesses and corporations don't make their employees take full advantage of their vacation time. Many studies have shown that employees (and owners, if you are self-employed) are far more productive when they take regular vacations. They are also happier and healthier, which leads to higher productivity in the long run.

But, back to you. When was the last time you took a full week of vacation? (By the way, going to spend a week with relatives does not count. As we all know, after a week with relatives, we need another week just to recover.)

Where did you go on vacation? What did you do? Did you stay in one place for a calm and leisurely respite? Or did you take one of those "25 Cities in Five Days" marathon trips? It doesn't matter which style you prefer, the question is, did you come back with more energy or less energy than when you left?

Today's technology makes it possible to never leave work. With cell phones, Blackberries, laptop computers, WIFI and wireless Internet connections, remote conferencing, and text messaging, it is possible to be 'on-the-job' every waking hour of your day, and available 24/7/365 if you don't mind being awakened during the night.

My question is, what is this drive to work 24/7 doing to our internal systems and our ability to take time to recharge our batteries, not to mention, time to have a life?

Technology has embedded itself more and more in our daily work environment. Many people tell me that technology has boosted their productivity. Frankly, I'm not convinced. Even if our productivity has increased, what has technology done for our personal well-being and our well-being at work? Has technology made us happier in our lives?

Two situations come to mind that make me question whether the benefits of technology outweigh the potential impacts on our vibrational systems, and our ability to stay focused and attract the life we want.

A business acquaintance asked me to play golf with him at a local country club. Tom has an insurance agency that specializes in insuring construction projects. These are usually multi-million dollar projects, often in other parts of the country and sometimes, in other parts of the world.

During the course of our round of golf, which lasted about six hours, Tom answered his cell phone to take a business-related call no less than seven times. In each instance, the game came to a halt while he dealt with some important detail of an insurance claim or policy. For me, and for the other two players in our foursome, the game took way too long, and the enjoyment of being outside, away from the office grind, was lost.

As I listened to Tom on the last call, it occurred to me that Tom did a disservice to himself, his playing partners...and his insurance client. He tried to be 'efficient' by playing golf and running his business at the same time. Unfortunately, Tom failed to give his full attention to either. His golf game was erratic (though he can play very well when he is focused on his game); his interaction with his playing partners was short and terse; and his attempt to handle the business issues, without all the important information at hand, irritated Tom and his clients.

There is an old saying that states: *"All work and no play make Jack a dull boy."*

I don't know about the 'dull' part, but Tom didn't enjoy himself, his work, the chance to recharge his batteries in the sunshine and fresh air, or the companionship of his playing partners. At the end of the round, he had a couple of stiff drinks to artificially calm himself, and then dashed back to work to deal with more problems.

Is this what life is supposed to be like? How can we expect to attract the life we really want, including the pleasure of spending quality time with friends and family, if our systems are overloaded with static we ourselves generate by always trying to do too much and always seeking...'more'?

The second situation related to technology that I see all too often is when a person becomes so self-important in his/her ego-driven-mind, that they believe their work and business cannot survive without their constant, minute-by-minute, micro-managed guidance.

You can easily identify one of these people. (By the way, if you are one of these people, don't let your ego-based mind take this as a criticism. Let your heart-based, inner-being simply take note that you may be creating a lot of the static that keeps you from attracting what you really want in life.)

The people I am thinking of have those crazy little wireless cell phones that wrap around your ear like an old hearing aid. There is a piece that goes around the ear to hold it on, an earplug with the speaker that goes in the ear, and a microphone extending out next to the cheek.

I must admit that it always unnerves me to walk down the street and pass a person who, for all practical purposes, seems to be talking to him/herself. Not only are they talking to themselves, they are fully animated, with hand gestures and facial expressions, and loud and varied pitches to their voices.

You know, in the old days, they used to wrap little white coats with very long arms around people like this and take them to a place referred to as 'The Funny Farm.' Every time I walk by a person like this, that image pops into my mind. I immediately give thanks that I don't hear little voices in my head.

I'm sorry, but no one is so important, no phone call is so important, that it can't wait until you can take the call in a reasonable place where you don't have to look like the village idiot when you talk. Does the President of the United States walk around with one of those little phones stuck in his ear? No, he doesn't. Is there anything you do in your job that is more important than the things the President does? Sorry, but I don't think so.

Now, lest you think I am making 'much ado about nothing', my point simply is that too often, we allow the world to impose it's ideas and demands upon us without thinking about the impact these things have on our ability to have a reasonable, happy life. We let ourselves be coerced into believing that the only way to exist in the world is by being accessible 24 hours a day, seven days a week, 365 days a year.

Is that really why we work so hard? Is that really what we want to attract? When do we allow ourselves time to recharge our batteries and actually experience life?

Everyone needs time off to clear the static from our systems and to remember why we work so hard. Otherwise, we just fool ourselves and believe that this chaotic existence is all that life has to offer.

Unless you <u>are</u> the Energizer Bunny, or unless you <u>are</u> in a hurry to come back as a hybrid vehicle, you might want to take it easy on that set of batteries you have inside of you. Taking good care of them is a lot easier than having to replace the whole car.

***

If being 'available' all the time suits your vibrational makeup, by all means, do what feels good. But, I suggest that you stop once in a while to consider what impact such a lifestyle has on your inner vibrations and your ability to have the life you really want.

33
I'm Going 'Green'

Is it because the glaciers are melting and the temperatures are rising that the world suddenly seems to be so focused on 'going green'? Everywhere you turn, companies are touting how they are going 'green' to do their part to slow global warming and to stop turning the planet into a toxic waste dump.

Don't get me wrong. I'm all in favor of the green movement. I'm even hopeful that we can start to turn things around so that the planet will still be viable when my daughter is my age.

I am a little disappointed, though, because all the emphasis is on going green in the areas of business, energy and the environment. There seems to be less focus on how we, as living, vibrating beings, can put a little more green in our lives. What does it mean to 'go green' on a personal level? It means we find ways to reduce the static the world seems bound and determined to overlay onto our personal vibrations.

Have you ever stopped to think about how the world we live in has changed vibrationally in the last 100 years? Nikola Tesla sent the first man-made, electronic radio signal transmission in 1893. (Even though Guglielmo Marconi was granted a patent for the radio in 1896 and is often given credit for the invention of the radio, it was Tesla who first demonstrated it. The patent rights were re-awarded to Tesla in 1943 after his death.)

Think about that. Until the year 1893, there were no man-made radio waves, no television transmissions, no microwave transmissions, no cell phone transmissions and no wireless communications of any kind. Now, only 116 years later, millions of radio stations and TV stations, and in excess of 3,000,000,000 (that's three BILLION) cell phones bombard us with their signals.

With a world population at the end of 2008 estimated at 6,740,600,000, almost 45% of the people on earth have a cell phone! Am I the only person who finds that hard to comprehend? I don't know about you, but I find this whole issue downright scary to think about. When we understand that we are vibrational beings, how could we not be impacted by all these transmissions?

Each of us has our own unique vibration, an energy fingerprint if you will. Every electronic transmission we come in contact with has the potential to impact our vibrations. What effect does this tsunami of electronic vibrations have on our ability to keep static out of our natural frequencies?

In addition to cell phones, most of us are exposed to low levels of electromagnetic radiation from our television screens and our computer monitors. Who knows what the long-term effect of exposure to these sources of transmissions might be on our DNA. (If I were a younger man thinking about having children, I might give serious consideration to buying some lead-lined underwear. And, yet, here I sit at my computer typing this book. Frankly, I'm surprised I don't glow in the dark when I go to bed at night.)

In 1987, 1,700,000 people were treated for depression in the U.S. By 2004, almost 10% of people over the age of 18 were being treated for depression, about 20,000,000 people. Is it just a coincidence that this huge increase in depression coincided with the rise in cell phone use from 11 million cell phones in 1987 to approximately 180 million by 2004? Kind of makes you wonder, doesn't it?

But, alas, cell phones, radios, TV's and computers are here to stay so we might as well get used to it. As the old saying goes, *"Don't waste time worrying about things you can't control."*

You do, however, have some control over how much exposure you get to some of these sources in your own home and office. The way I see it, any reduction I can make in the amount of exposure I get from electronic devices and other sources of pollution, the more chance I will be able to keep my own vibrations clear.

If you want to think about 'going green' for yourself, here are a couple of ideas to consider.

- Keep some live plants in your home and office. It's a proven fact that they absorb pollutants, produce oxygen, and they, too, are alive. If you talk nicely to your plants, maybe they will return the favor.
- Reduce the amount of time you watch TV and work at a computer.
- Consider buying a negative ion generator. Negative ions are part of the reason why the air smells so fresh around the ocean and waterfalls. Both produce negative ions. Ion generators can help eliminate pollen, mold spores, dust, pet dander and many other allergy causing particulates from the air you breath.
- Drink filtered water. Notice that I didn't say bottled water. Many brands of bottled water, especially those that use plastic containers, contain more pollutants and dangerous metals than tap water.
- Eat foods that are high in antioxidants. Think

of antioxidants as mini-black holes that suck up dangerous particles called free radicals. Some scientists believe that free radicals are the primary cause of age-related diseases.
- Exercise. I would recommend taking a walk in the fresh air but finding 'fresh' air can be a real problem nowadays. Anyway, exercise will help your body dump the toxins it accumulates from the environment, food, shampoo, makeup, toothpaste…well, you get the idea. (Most things have stuff in them that is unpronounceable; and too many things have stuff in them that will cause cancer if taken in large enough doses.)
- Get some natural sunshine for 10-20 minutes a day. Hey, we evolved spending time in the sun. I seriously doubt that our bodies have forgotten what some good old-fashioned sunshine, in limited amounts, can do to brighten our spirits.

I admit that none of these things is revolutionary or likely to be a panacea for the static thrust upon us by our environment. But, every little bit counts.

***

The more static you can eliminate from your surroundings, the clearer you can keep your own vibrations. Pay attention to your environment, the foods you eat, the water you drink, and the air you breathe. Reduce your exposure to electronic devices and pollutants as much as possible. The body you have is the only one you get. Take care of it, and it will help you attract the life you want.

34
Having to Change Is a Royal Pain in the Butt!

When people hear the word 'change', they often experience a negative feeling. Why is that? If there is one thing that is constant in life, it is the fact that things change. Whether we care to admit it or not, change is the reason we are here. Without changes to our RNA/DNA (mutations is such a negative word), we might still be one-celled organisms.

Nevertheless, for many people, change is a pain in the butt.

"Why can't things just stay the same? Why do I have to change my life to suit others? Why do I have to get old? Why do I have to move to another city, get a different job, find a new relationship?"

On the other hand, we welcome some changes. Interestingly, these can be the same changes that we feel threatened by under different circumstances.

"I'm really looking forward to moving to a new city, getting a new job, and finding a new partner."

Strange, yes? But, true nevertheless.
So, why do we tend to have a basic negative feeling toward

change? The reason may be that in the past, many of the changes we found disagreeable were changes that we felt were forced upon us, changes that were not of our own choosing. This can certainly be true when as children we were not in control of our lives.

"Do this, don't do that. Change your clothes, change that bad attitude, change your friends, we're moving to a new city and leaving all your friends behind."

Thus, there is a tendency that develops when we are young to associate the word 'change' with bad things and bad feelings. We often continue to associate the word 'change' with bad feelings right on into adulthood.

If we look at our lives from a more objective viewpoint, we can see that we are changing all the time. Good changes and bad changes. The primary difference seems to be that changes we view as something we 'have to do', things that are dictated by others in which we feel we have no choice or say in the matter, are usually viewed negatively. On the other hand, things that we decide to change for ourselves, we are more likely to view positively.

When we put the concepts behind attraction into practice, we will be confronted with change. We will have to change the way we think and act. For many of us, the second we hear the word 'change', our old definition of change (change generally means bad things) jumps in and the next thought that comes to mind is:

"I DON'T WANT TO! Who are you to tell me I have to change? I like being miserable. Leave me alone. Nothing good ever comes from having to change."

Unfortunately, as the concept of attraction dictates, we just end up attracting more negative changes. Bummer.

Science teaches us that everything in the Universe vibrates, albeit it at many different frequencies. We, too, have a frequency that we are born with. Depending on your belief system, you might think of this frequency as your soul, your inner being, or perhaps, your personal vibration. Regardless of what we call it, the fact is that we all have a vibrational frequency that more or less defines who we are.

Our problems start to arise when the pure harmonic tone that we are born with gets interference in the form of static. It is like a radio. If our personal frequency is 610, we are not set up to receive or transmit frequencies that are at 609 or 611. Those other frequencies produce 'static' on our internal stations.

Of course, much like fingerprints, it is doubtful that any two individuals vibrate at exactly the same frequency. Thus, the best we can hope for is to keep our own frequency tuned with as little static from others as possible. We become at odds with our internal frequencies when we allow others to impinge on our frequencies. In truth, however, others cannot create static for us unless we allow them to. Similarly, we cannot create static in other people unless they let us.

Of equal importance is the fact that no one else can tune the static out of our frequency for us. How could they? They don't know, feel, or experience our exact frequency. There is no way they can know when we have tuned out the static on our personal station. They can't truly know when we feel good.

As children (and for many of us as adults) we don't understand any of this frequency stuff. We do know, however, when something doesn't feel right. Unfortunately, we are vulnerable to the static others produce in our vicinity. The impact of that static can pack a wallop that knocks us off our frequency.

Often, when we are told by a parent or an elder that we 'should' do something, they tell us to do what is in harmony with their personal frequencies. Since they don't know our personal frequency (nor often their own, for that matter), their attempts to help us just create more static.

When our parents, teachers, and elders fiddle around with our tuners while we are children, it feels like they are trying to change who we are. Their tuning frequently creates more static in our systems. When they tell us to change, it creates more static, and it feels bad.

Many of us carry these thoughts/feelings into adulthood. When our spouse, friend, boss, or relative tries to fine-tune us so that we sound good to them, it generates more static in our systems.

The more static it creates, the worse it feels, the more we rebel, and the more negative static we produce. This, of course, just makes everyone feel worse. What happens next? Others try even harder to tune us to their frequencies, and vice versa. It is a vicious cycle that seldom ends in good vibrations for anyone.

The point I want to make is that the concept of change has negative connotations for many people. In the past we probably ended up with more static and feeling worse for the effort.

I would like to create a new vision for the concept of change. Let's accept for a moment that we are born with a specific frequency, our own, personal frequency that feels natural and good to us.

Let's also consider that this frequency is the essence of who we are, and that our inner self or inner being, stays the same throughout our lives. What we think, believe, or do might change a bit from time to time, but the base frequency of who we are stays the same, unique to us.

Consider the idea that the purpose of change is to reduce our static. Let us think of change as a way to re-tune our internal systems to their original, static-free frequencies. From this perspective, we never have to, nor should we try to, change our frequency to something we aren't. We should never change our natural frequency to meet the needs of someone else. The only thing that will ultimately make us feel good is to do what we can to keep our personal frequencies clear of static, just like they were when we were born.

When we read books or attend lectures and someone tells us that we need to make changes if we want to lead happy and fulfilling lives, don't use the old definition of change. Don't ever believe that you have to change who you are to meet the needs and match the frequencies of others. The only changes you should consider are those that will help you remove static from your system. The only changes worth making are ones that return you to being that good-feeling, pure-toned person you really are.

Would you be willing to invest your thoughts, your time, your energy, and your beliefs in changes that return you to that pure tone that is your natural vibration, one that feels good and pleasing? I think you would.

Change is not our enemy unless it increases the static in our systems. Change that re-tunes us to our natural frequencies always feels good. It is only the static that makes us feel bad.

When I discussed this idea of change with a friend, he raised an interesting question.

"If we all have our own personal and unique frequency, how can we ever hope to have close relationships with another person? Our

frequencies will never perfectly match those of any other person. So, aren't we doomed to have static?"

The easiest way I can think about this is to think of frequencies in terms of music. Music is a vibration that we hear with our ears. But, it is just that…a vibration. Music has a different frequency than we do. However, in music we know… we can hear…when two (or more) different frequencies sound good together. We say that those frequencies are in harmony with each other.

The concept of attraction allows us to attract things and people who, even though they do not have our exact frequency, are in close harmony with us and who allow us to produce pleasing sounds, feelings, and vibrations together. We have often heard someone say: *"Don't they go well together?"* This is just another way to say that our vibrations are in harmony. Our vibrations create more harmony than static.

Whether it is a lover, a spouse, a relative, a close friend, a co-worker, or a boss, most of us know when we vibrate well with another person. We also know when we are around people who make us feel a lot of static in our systems. It is in our best interest to avoid people who don't vibrate in harmony with us.

Please recognize that even though another person has a different frequency that doesn't harmonize with ours, it doesn't mean they are a 'bad' person. It just means that they are on a different frequency that is not in harmony with ours.

When you realize that you don't vibrate well with another person, avoiding or distancing yourself from that person may be the best option. If you try to change your frequency to match theirs, it will only increase your static. On the other hand, if you try to get them to change their frequency to match yours, it will only increase their static. Neither of these is a good solution.

This creates a real problem when you find yourself in a situation that puts you in frequent and close proximity to a person with whom you don't vibrate well. If you don't vibrate well with your boss, what can you do? The best solution is to interact with that person as little as possible. In addition, it would be useful to focus your thoughts, desires and beliefs to attract a new boss or a new job with co-workers who vibrated more in harmony with you.

This doesn't mean that you should quit your job. If you lost your source of income you would not feel good either. Change for the sake of change doesn't accomplish anything. Effective change requires a careful balance that limits or reduces static in the current situation while you make a conscious effort to attract a better situation.

If you focus on how bad your situation is, attraction will bring you more of the bad situation. Fortunately, the more you focus on attracting a better situation, the sooner it will have the opportunity to manifest itself.

The same is true for a situation involving a relative, a close friend or even a spouse. One might ask:

"How did I get together with my spouse in the first place? While we seemed to vibrate in harmony when we first got together, it seems that we are no longer compatible. How did that happen? Doesn't that mean that one of us changed our frequency during the time we have been together?"

It might be that two people who no longer vibrate well together may have tried hard to re-tune or match their vibrations when they were first getting to know each other. One or both may have attempted to change their personal frequencies to make the relationship work.

We have a base frequency that does not change during our lifetime. Any actions we take to force our frequency to be different creates static in our systems. The harder we try to change our frequency to something that we aren't, the worse the static becomes. At that point, it is hard to remember and feel our unique frequency.

Have you ever heard someone say:

"I just don't seem to know who I am any more? I don't seem to know who the real me is."

This is likely to be a person who has tried or been forced to change their basic frequency to one that is unnatural. Some people can't figure out who they really are because they can't hear their original tone through all the static. The good news is, their original frequency is still there. It may be buried, but the desire to reassert itself still exists.

At the start of this chapter I mentioned three thoughts related to our frequencies and static:

1. People cannot create static in us unless we let them.

2. We cannot create static in other people unless they let us.

3. No one else can tune the static out of our frequency for us.

If we do not attract the people, experiences, and feelings into our lives that we want, there is a good chance that we have allowed a lot of static to drown out our personal frequencies and vibrations. The first steps to remedy this problem are (a) decide what we want; (b) put our thoughts, desires and actions behind those wants; and (c) allow our feelings to tell us when we are moving toward what we want.

When we feel bad, we are not moving toward what we want and we are creating more static in our system. The more we focus on the static, the more static we will attract. The more we focus on what we want, the better we will feel and the more we will vibrate to attract what we want.

***

If you have trouble attracting what you want, try to figure out what caused the static and distance yourself from it as much as possible. Focus your thoughts on what you do want and intend to attract the people, ideas, thoughts and feelings that will let your true vibration ring loud and clear.

35
Misery Loves Company

Some of the people I talk to say it is hard to begin to get their 'it' together. They say that at the beginning of the process, they often don't notice any difference in their ability to attract what they want.

From a purely logical standpoint, this makes sense. If we have spent a number of years (or, in some cases, much of our lives) coming from a place of not having, we have a lot of history pushing us along that path. It is unlikely that we can quickly change all those past thoughts and habits.

However, the sooner we experience small changes in our ability to attract a new and better life, the sooner we will put more of our beliefs and energy behind our natural vibrations to attract what we want.

It is important that we recognize when we <u>are</u> attracting what we want; otherwise, we will never turn ourselves around in the direction we want to go. The more we surround ourselves with things that vibrate in harmony with our own personal frequencies, the sooner we will notice that we feel better more of the time.

Most of us spend a significant amount of time in the presence of other people. Each of these people has his/her own vibration. Unfortunately, many of them do not know what they want, and they have allowed their vibrations to become overloaded with static.

Whether these people are family members, co-workers, friends, or just random people we encounter, when we are in their presence, we will feel their vibrations just as they feel ours. If we are not strong in our beliefs about what we want, and if we are not vigilant in keeping our personal frequencies free of static, we can be bumped off our natural frequency by people who are not in harmony with our true desires.

The old saying "Misery Loves Company" describes how easy it is to allow static into our lives, especially static from people who, quite honestly, are more miserable than we are.

Have you ever been around a person or a group of people who are discussing 'how terrible things are right now?' The subject might be the state of the world, the state of their health, the state of their finances, the state of their relationships, or the state of their job/career. Talk about a downer. The vibrations associated with these discussions are negative enough to stop an elephant in its tracks.

These vibrations are made more powerful when a group of people vibrate together and contribute to the same negative frequency. A perfect example of this tendency happens when we attend a funeral. What is the mood?...Black.

Now, I'm not suggesting that people should be happy and joyous at a funeral. I am simply using this example as a way for you to experience how negative vibrations resonate together, with either positive or negative implications.

I always liked the idea of the Irish 'wake' after a funeral. While the funeral itself was solemn, after the funeral, friends and family gathered together to celebrate the good things and the good times they remembered with the deceased. A little liquid libation helped lighten the mood toward the good-feeling side of the ledger.

Unfortunately, in situations such as a funeral (around a bunch of unhappy coworkers, in the midst of feuding relatives, etc.), if we are not careful, we can be knocked out of the static-free frequencies that we have worked so hard to achieve. The more bummed-out the group is, the harder it is to stay focused and static free.

So, it is time to ask yourself a question. How much time do you spend around people who are heavily invested in the negative aspects of their lives? Do you have to spend a lot of time around people who bitch, moan, and complain about how bad life is?

Ah, misery does love company. Since most people don't understand how important it is to work to attract what they really want in their lives, they get what they don't want by default. When these people encounter someone who does understand and who works with conscious intention to get his/her 'it' together, their first reaction is to do their best to convert that person into a bummed-out naysayer. Misery so loves company.

People who are not happy (which we all may be at various points in our lives) get irritated when confronted with someone who has his/her 'it' together. It pisses them off when someone else is living the life they would like to be living.

Since many of us have not thought about and decided what we really want out of life, we have trouble focusing positive thoughts toward what we want. Too often, we end up focused on what we don't want, what we don't have, and we allow ourselves to be influenced by those around us, most of whom are not any happier than we are.

If you really want to start getting your 'it' together, you will make far more progress if you don't have to climb over a lot of 'naysayer mountains' on the way.

Now, some of you may be thinking that you don't have a lot of control over who you interact with, especially at home or at work. While it may be true that you can't just leave home or quit your job, don't use that as a cop out. That rationalization will do nothing to help you change your life and begin to attract what you really want.

Every minute that you spend either by yourself or in the company of other forward-thinking people is a minute that gets you closer to what you want. You are in control of your time. Part of the process of getting your 'it' together is to decide which people you wish to spend your time with. If you leave it to the universe to guess what type of people to send your way, you probably won't like what you get.

Think about this for a moment. Do you really like being around someone who bitches, moans and complains, and who usually blames someone else for his/her troubles, taking no responsibility for the mess they made of their life? No, of course you don't. And, in truth, neither does anyone else. We would all like to be around happy, friendly, like-minded people.

<u>Happy, friendly people want to be around other happy, friendly people.</u> So, if you want to attract friendly people into your life, what is the best way to do that? By being a bummed-out, burned-out, stressed-out Grinch? Sorry, wrong answer.

When we think about who we attract into our lives, you will often see that like <u>does</u> attract like. If we're negative-acting, negative-thinking, miserable-feeling human beings, we attract more of the same. Misery <u>loves</u> company.

But, the good news is, happiness also loves company. People who try to get their 'it' together with conscious intent are likely to attract people who are also trying to get their 'it' together. The positive vibrations that build in a room full of forward-looking, like-minded individuals can resonate together into a crescendo of good feelings.

If you are not attracting what you want in your life, and if you find you spend too much time around bummed-out, burned-out people, remember...you have the power to change the choices you make. You have the power to choose to spend time with people who share your desire to get their 'it' together.

The sooner you get yourself away from the naysayers and into the company of forward thinkers, the quicker you will be able to turn your life around and change into the person you want to be. It's your choice. What kind of people do you want to spend the rest of your life with?

***

Make the conscious choice to focus your beliefs, energies and intentions on <u>being</u> the kind of person you want to attract into your life. If you do, you may soon find yourself surrounded by a wonderful group of like-minded enthusiasts.

36
Are You For or Against?

As we work to move forward toward the life we want, it is easy to lapse into old habits. Therefore it's important to remember that the more we focus on positive progress, the more likely we are to attract the good feelings we seek.

Unfortunately, we are often confronted with situations and people who vibrate negatively. One of the ways I help myself steer clear of these negative emitters is to assess whether they are 'For' something or 'Against' something.

In previous chapters, I discussed how certain words create negative vibrations. Words like 'change', 'want', and 'attract' can cause unconscious reactions that attract more static.

Words that come from the base words of 'No' or 'Not' are more likely to create negative vibrations than words that come from a feeling of 'Yes'. Let me give a couple of examples of how 'No-based' words can lead us down the wrong vibrational path.

Have you ever heard of the organization called MADD? The letters stand for 'Mothers Against Drunk Drivers'. The intent and focus of this organization is certainly a worthy cause. I have no respect for people who endanger themselves and others because of their uncontrolled drinking habits.

Unfortunately, from a standpoint of attraction, what are these mothers likely to attract based on the name of their organization? Sadly, I think they are likely to attract more drunk drivers.

Notice how the word 'Against' puts a negative vibration on this issue. These mothers are mad at drunk drivers who have caused injury and death to their children. They are angry, upset, emotional and depressed. These are reasonable feelings and emotions that we would all experience if a child of ours was injured or killed by a drunk driver.

However, the question is, what kind of vibrations are these mothers emitting and attracting when they come from these negative emotions?

What if the name of the organization was 'GLAD'? Instead of being against drunk drivers, what if these mothers were 'for' sober drivers? What vibrations would they emit (and attract) if they placed their emphasis on teaching the positive benefits of moderate drinking?

Do these women really want to teach adults and children to be MADD at drunk drivers? Wouldn't it perhaps be better to teach them to be glad and thankful and appreciative of sober drivers?

Can you feel the vibrational difference within you when you think of being 'for' something versus being 'against' something. For me, the thought of being 'for' something focuses my attention on moving forward to the goal I want to attain. When I think about being 'against' something, it focuses me on the past, on what isn't right, on what I don't have.

A friend of mine told me that her life works best when she focuses on moving toward what feels good, and moving away from what feels bad. She talked about a situation at the school where she teaches. The teachers and the school board were locked in a battle over salaries, tenure, vacation days, health care benefits, etc.

Many of the more vocal teachers complained about what they weren't getting. The school board simultaneously declared that they could never provide the kind of benefits the teachers wanted. *"I don't have;" "You can't have."* No, no, no. The negative vibrations got so intense that it was a wonder the two sides ever got together.

In situations like these, one technique that negotiators use to get the two sides to calm down is to impose a 'cooling off period'. Neither side meets to discuss the issue for 10—30 days as a way to let tempers cool, and to allow calmer minds to prevail. In these situations, it may be the best way to bring the negative vibrations down to a point where reasonable discussions can take place.

The same situations can be found at home. Parents have learned the technique of 'time outs' for their kids. The child goes and sits in a quiet place to let their vibrations and emotions calm down. In truth, of course, the same is true for the parents. This 'time out' period allows the parents to get their vibrations under control, to refocus on what is really important, their children, and to look for positive ways to move forward.

I discussed these ideas with a person who said: *"That is all well and good, but you can't always just run away or ask for a 'time out' when you find yourself in the middle of a fight."* And, he is right. We can't always run for the door when a spouse or a boss or a stranger unleashes a negative volley at us.

However, if we don't consciously think about what we want; if we don't pay attention and focus on doing things we are for (instead of things we are against), we may frequently find ourselves in these unpleasant situations. Even worse, attraction is likely to bring us even more of these negative situations.

What organizations do you belong to? What kind of people do you hang around with? What 'causes' do you support?

Are these organizations and people 'for' something? Are they focused on the positive things they want to accomplish, or are they mostly focused on what they don't want others to do? You can't expect to attract the positive aspects of the life you seek if you surround yourself with negative people who are always taking a negative position.

***

Focus on what you are 'for'. The more you focus on moving forward toward the positive things you want, the more likely you are to attract the situations and people who are working toward a similar, positive outcome.

37
Conflict Resolution

When we focus our attention on what we want, the people around us aren't always thrilled with the idea or the result. As we move toward fulfilling our wants, some of those wants may be different from the things the people around us want. When this occurs, conflicts can arise.

This is not a book about conflict resolution. That is a very broad topic in its own right and you can find many good books on the subject. If you find that you have disagreements with co-workers, loved ones, or just casual acquaintances, I suggest that you look for other sources of information to guide you in your resolution process.

However, I do want to mention something that might help you scale down the negative intensity of these interactions. I find it useful to keep in mind when I encounter people whose vibrations don't resonate well with my own.

We seem to live in a very bi-polar world. Pick just about any topic or issue and you will find that there are a lot of black and white feelings around many issues. There are often extreme thoughts and beliefs with seemingly few gray areas of compromise in the middle.

If you think about issues like politics, religion, sex, marriage, abortion, big business, and war, you will find that the world is split by those who are for something, and those who are against it. When it comes to people, these situations often digress into a position best stated as, "You're either with us, or you're against us."

I'm not sure why or how humanity got itself into such a position of extremes. When you step back from some of the issues and try to take an objective look at them, the differences are often not as extreme as we might believe.

When you look at a marriage or a friendship, we already know that both people have their own unique vibrational frequency. No two frequencies will match exactly. So, by definition, there are going to be some areas where two people are not in agreement. What unfortunately happens is that small and often insignificant things can overwhelm a relationship to the point that we find ourselves in a position of 'me against you'.

The concept of attraction says that 'like attracts like'. In a marriage or friendship, there must have been a number of things on which the two individuals were originally in vibrational harmony, or else they would probably never have found each other in the first place.

The trouble usually starts when two individuals or groups focus on the little things they don't agree on and, in the process, they forget all the hundreds of things on which they do agree. As more and more focus and attention is given to the differences, attraction brings more differences. Soon, a terrible storm gathers momentum in a downward spiral of negative feelings.

With that in mind, I want to offer a little visual and physical tool that might help us remember that our differences are often few, and our similarities many.

In a conflict, there are two sides to the fight or issue: I'm for it, you're against it; I believe this, you believe the opposite;

I think that something belongs to me; you believe it should be yours. Two opposite sides.

When we think about global conflicts like war, we can see whole countries that are divided by some invisible line that designates the boundary between what's mine and what's yours. In extreme cases, a huge wall may actually be built to make sure you stay on your side of the fence. There may be hundreds of miles of land behind me and behind you on our respective sides of the fence.

Everything and everyone on my side is against you, and vice versa. With that picture in mind, it's difficult to expect that we could ever get past our differences and find some room for compromise.

Now, let me give you a slightly different image of the two sides of an issue. Reach in your pocket or purse and pull out a penny. That penny represents the two opposite sides of an issue. Heads…you're for it; tails…you're against it.

Now, have another person stand right in front of you. That person represents 'THEM'. You represent "US'. Here's what I want you to do. (By the way, if there isn't another person around with whom you can do this experiment, just imagine doing it in your mind.)

Take the penny and hold it in front of you with one hand. Hold it between your thumb and index finger. Hold the coin vertically so that the two sides of the coin are facing towards you and the other person, heads toward you, tails toward them. I then want each of you to take the index finger of your other hand and place it on the side of the coin facing each of you.

Both individuals should put pressure against the tip of their index finger on their side of the coin until you can release your hold on the coin. The coin will stay in place, being held there by the pressure of each person's index finger pushing against the coin and the pressure being applied by the other person's finger.

You now have a representation of two people on opposite sides of an issue. If one pushes harder, the other person will push back even harder, so as not to 'give in'. The harder each side pushes, the harder the other side has to push back to keep things in a state of status quo.

Now, here is what I want you to consider. While it is true that you are on opposite sides of the coin, and even though you seem to be at opposite ends of the issue, and even though there seems like there is nothing that could ever bring you together, the truth is, you are only the width of the coin apart in your positions.

In reality, we are often only the tiniest distance apart, and that tiny distance is all we have to traverse to come together and reach a solution. In most cases, the wall between us really isn't hundreds of feet thick. On many issues, we could be just a fraction of an inch away from a mutually agreeable resolution.

But, how can we get to a place where we might find such a compromise. The best way to lower the wall is for both sides to back off a little and ease off on the pressure. If you do this with your partner, as soon as you both ease off the pressure on your index fingers, the coin will fall to the floor, and it will no longer be a barrier to resolving the problem.

As we focus our attention on what we want to attract into our lives, there will be times when what we want may not be what a spouse, a partner or a friend may want. When little things are allowed to escalate into major issues, both sides end up pushing harder and a barrier forms. This barrier can block out everything we work so hard to attract.

***

As you move forward and decide what you want in your life, and as you implement your plan, don't let little issues prevent you from getting what you want. Remember that the wall between you and another person may be no thicker than the width of a penny. When both sides ease off, that tiny barrier can disappear and allow both sides to get what they want.

38
Grumpy Employees Attract Grumpy Customers

As we make conscious efforts to distance ourselves from people with whom we don't vibrate well, we may notice that there are certain businesses where we don't feel well-treated on a vibratory level. Just as we want to be conscious of the TV shows we watch and the books we read, where we do business sends messages to our subconscious minds about the kind of people we want to attract into our lives.

Can you think of a business that has friendly, helpful employees? Do you know a waitress, salesperson or receptionist who makes you feel good when you enter the front door? Have you noticed how nice it feels when a real, live, friendly, human being answers the phone when you call a company to ask a question?

There are always at least two parties to a sale, the vendor and the customer. Both parties have their own unique vibrations that they bring to the transaction. If you work for a company or own one, you often play the part of the vendor. If you do not work, then you participate in these interactions as the customer. Regardless of which role you play (the roles can switch depending on whether you are buying or selling), the question I want you think about is, why would anyone want to do business with a company where the employees are grumpy?

I see this problem often when I consult with businesses. I call the company to set up an appointment and the person who answers the phone <u>is</u> The Creature from the Black Lagoon. The phone is answered with all the warmth and enthusiasm of a brick. The basic vibrational tone which is conveyed is:

"Yeah? Whadaya want? Can't you see I'm busy here? I have work to do. I can't be bothered with having to deal with a stupid customer."

You know the type. How does that make you feel when someone answers the phone that way? Are you excited about doing business with that person or company? NOT! Thanks, but I think I'll take my business elsewhere.

If you pay attention when you go to a business, from the moment you enter the front door you can feel whether the employees enjoy their work. Unfortunately, since the majority of polled workers say they don't like their job (these being many of the same people who haven't consciously decided what they want in life), your chances of finding a business with a bunch of happy employees are pretty low. Nevertheless, there are varying levels of dissatisfaction, and, occasionally, you may come across a business where the employees actually seem to be enjoying themselves.

The concept of attraction operates from the premise that like attracts like. Thus, a business staffed with grumpy employees is more likely to attract grumpy customers. Remember: *"Misery loves company."* One might also say that *"Misery loves companies."* If we are grumpy managers, we will attract grumpy employees. Eavesdrop on the conversation around the water cooler for a couple of minutes and you can get a feel for whether the employees are 'for' the company, or 'against' it.

There is an excellent book called *"The No Complaining Rule"* by Jon Gordon which offers some great ideas and insight about ways to overcome the negative vibrations caused by chronic complaining amongst employees. I recommend you read it if you own or manage a business with more than a handful of employees.

In my own work with companies, I suggest a way for employees to share their thoughts and grievances that can help prevent the negative-complaint- train from getting out of control. Here is how this simple system works.

When an employee has a problem or a complaint, they bring it to management's attention in the following way. First, they put the complaint in writing. This accomplishes two things: (1) it forces the employee to stop and think about what they want to say; and (2) it makes them realize they must put it into written form. Minor problems often disappear when the employee knows s/he will have to take the time to write the problem down.

The second thing the employee must do is propose a realistic solution to the problem. No more venting just to let off steam. If the problem is real, the employee who experiences the problem is familiar enough with it to offer a possible solution.

The third and final part of this system is the more difficult piece. That piece is: *"If you don't wish to follow this system, don't complain at all."* Negative comments, accusations, gossip, and water-cooler-talk will no longer be tolerated. Negativity ruins morale, reduces productivity, and forces all employees to have to put up with the negative vibrations of a few grump-butts. And, in the end, it attracts grumpy customers.

When you are in the role of the customer, how you vibrate also impacts the kind of employees you will attract. If you go into a business having a bad day, in a hurry, tired and grumpy, the odds are, you will soon find yourself talking to your mirror image in the form of a disgruntled employee.

If, on the other hand, you walk in with a smile on your face and a friendly *"Hello"*, there is a good chance you will attract a fellow human being who would love to help someone who is working at getting his/her it together. Remember: *"Happiness also loves company."*

The way I look at it, when I go into a store, it's my money I'm spending. I deserve to be treated like a decent, doing-the-best-I-can person, who is working at getting his 'it' together, and who is trying to add as little static to the world (and my life), as I can. Why would I want to sabotage my efforts by doing business with companies whose employees vibrate like Darth Vader? Thanks, but no thanks. I'll take my life and business elsewhere.

Our subconscious minds never rest. They work 24/7/365 to filter out unneeded information based on the conscious (and unconscious) instructions we give them. Anytime you can reduce the amount of static you must deal with during your day-to-day activities, the clearer the message you send to your subconscious. By sending a clear, consistent message, you are more likely to attract what you want and the sort of people you want in your life.

***

We do not attract only during certain times of the day or only in certain places. We attract things, people, and situations, either by design or by default, all the time. We can't relax our focus on what we want when we are at work, when we are buying groceries at the local supermarket, or at any other time or place. If you don't want to attract grumpy employees, grumpy coworkers, or grumpy people in general, don't tell your subconscious it's okay to be around those types of people.

39
The IDM File

One of the problems that I have with books that help us get our lives together is that they seldom provide me with real-life ways to get out of feeling bad once I am already down in the dumps. I admit, I'm not much for filling out worksheets, meditating, or 'going inside myself' as a way to let go of bad feelings. I always end up asking *"But, what can I actually DO right now to get myself headed back in the right direction?"*

I found too many books that described getting our 'it' together as an easy process...'all you have to do is change the way you think.' Easy for them maybe, but I never found it easy at all.

Therefore, I experimented with ways to get unstuck when I found myself in a bad-feeling or seriously-irritated funk. I talked about some of these ideas in previous chapters: thinking of myself as a black hole; dumping the past to make way for the new; using specific words to express forward movement. Hopefully, one of these has given you a way to start moving towards what you want.

There are times, however, when I have found myself wallowing in the mud of a recent situation. Usually it was after someone did something to me that I thought was unjust. For those times when I am in the midst of a bad feeling, more drastic measures may be needed. Here is one of the more proactive actions I use to let go of the past and move on. I call it the IDM File.

'IDM' stands for *"It Don't Matter."*

NOTE: I realize that there are some of you who thought: *"That's not right. To be grammatically correct, it should read 'It Doesn't Matter.'"*

You're right, of course. But let me ask you a question. Does the fact that it doesn't say *"It Doesn't Matter"*...really matter in the process of getting your 'it' together? I doubt it.

Why is this such a big deal? Because we all get in the bad habit of focusing our attention on stuff that really doesn't matter. And, when we are focused on stuff that 'don't matter', when we give our attention to stuff that has no chance of getting us closer to what we want, we aren't focused on what we really want.

This brings me back to the IDM file. When I'm upset, when I feel like crap, or when I want to wring someone's neck, I identify why I feel this way, and then I file the whole thing in the IDM file.

Let's say you are at work and your boss or a co-worker goes ballistic on you. They read you the riot act for something you didn't do, or for something over which you had absolutely no control. To make matters worse, you feel that you can't say much back to them for fear you might lose your job.

How are you feeling? Angry? Frustrated? Pissed? Whipped on? Berated? Ridiculed? Ready to punch the person's lights out?

What? You thought you were the only person who has those kinds of emotions and feelings? Hardly! You might remember that according to the Bible, even God got seriously irritated a time or two. Once He even sent a big flood to straighten things out a bit. Hey, if getting a little upset is good enough for God, I figure it's good enough for me.

We're only human. We have emotions and feelings. That's just the way it is. But, that is not a bad thing. It is a wonderful thing. The worse the feeling is, the more likely we are to recognize that we are not focused on what we want.

It is not bad to feel emotions! Emotions and the feelings that go along with them are messengers. It's their job to tell us when we've gotten off track and when we are not focused on our wants.

It doesn't mean you are a bad person if you feel anger or frustration any more than feeling love makes you a good person. They are just emotions telling us to pay attention and focus on getting our 'it' together.

So, there you are at work (at home, in traffic, stuck in line at the grocery store, etc.), feeling seriously irritated at life. Now what?

Here is what I do. First, get away from the situation as soon as you can and get to a place where you can vent your feelings without attracting attention. You might even have to wait until you get home from work to deal with the really big stuff. Regardless, get to a place where you can gather your thoughts alone.

Now, get out a pad of paper and write down how you feel and why you feel that way.

"I'm really pissed! That stupid moron wouldn't know a good piece of work if it bit him in the ass! Who does she think she is treating me that way? I've a good mind to go tell her where she can stick her stupid report!"

Let it all hang out. If you are somewhere that you can yell, then yell. Throw a tantrum. Scream. Curse. Blow off some steam before you rupture a pipe. (However, I don't recommend punching a wall or a file cabinet. Inflicting pain on yourself is <u>not</u> going to make you feel better.)

Whether or not you take the opportunity to yell, make sure you write down the emotions you are feeling on a piece of paper. Then, once you have let out some of the major steam, sit down, calm yourself, take pleasure in crumpling the piece of paper up into a tight little ball, and then throw the piece of paper into the IDM file, otherwise known as…the wastebasket.

Why? Because nothing you can do about that bad situation really matters in getting you what you want. IDM.

Will this process get rid of a bad boss or a stupid co-worker? No. Will it help you get rid of a crazy in-law, a worthless friend, or a cheating spouse? No. But, the truth is, nothing you can do at that moment will accomplish those wishes either. And <u>no amount of time being irritated at the situation will get you closer to what you want.</u>

The purpose of this little exercise is to get you to notice your bad feelings, give them thanks for bringing the unpleasantness of the situation to your full attention (at the top of your lungs, if necessary), and then redirect your thoughts, energies and intentions to go forward toward what you do want. Write down how you feel and then throw that bad feeling in the trash. Be done with it and move on. IDM.

***

When a situation is bad enough to raise your hackles, you may have to do something to clear out the negative vibrations of the situation before you can make enough room to replace them with the positive vibrations of what you want to attract.

Then, refocus on what you do want and direct your energies, intentions, and vibrations on attracting what you do want.

No amount of focusing on what you don't want will ever bring you what you do want.

40
Making a List and Checking It Twice

Because I like to keep things simple, I did not include any worksheets or tests or questionnaires to fill out in this book. Frankly, I find that the mere mention of the word 'list' often generates negative vibrations for many people. Perhaps it comes from that old phrase about Santa Claus who is *"Making a list, checking it twice, going to find out who's naughty or nice."*

Bah, humbug! Anyway, I think this is the only time I am going to ask you to make a list. So, if you happen to be a person who reacts negatively to the thought of making a list...GET OVER IT! It's for your own good! (Whoa, there's a phrase that will create chills from the past.)

The bad news is, it's a huge list. You will probably need ten or twenty reams of paper to complete this list. And what does this list comprise? It is a list of all the things you <u>don't</u> want in life.

Yes, that's right. I want you to make a list of the things you don't want to attract into your life. Let me give you a few items from my personal list as examples.

- I do not want to be a window washer on skyscrapers.
- I do not want to spend four hours commuting to and from work.
- I do not want to have a job that appears on the TV show "*Dirty Jobs.*"

- I do not want to be a belly dancer.
- I do not want to attach tags to mattresses that read "*Do not remove this tag under penalty of law.*"
- I do not want to marry my cousin's mother's sister's daughter.
- I do not want to teach pigs to sing (it accomplishes nothing and really irritates the pig.)
- I do not want to be in politics.
- I do not want to be around politicians.
- I do not want to know any politicians.

(By the way, do you know the difference between a catfish and a politician? One is a bottom-dwelling, scum sucker. The other is a fish)

Anyway, I'm sure you get the gist of this. But, as you can see, this could end up being a very long list.

"*Why,*" you might ask, "*would I want to make such a list? It could take me the rest of my life to complete such a list. If I spend all my time writing down what I don't want, how will I have time to focus on what I do want?*"

Dang. You're a lot smarter than I thought you were. I thought maybe I could slip this by you, but no. I can see that you're way too smart for that.

However, I would like to pose a question. Is there any possibility that this is exactly what you have been doing for some/much/most of your life? Maybe you didn't write these things down, but is there any chance that you spent a lot of time thinking about what you didn't want instead of thinking about what you do want?

Yeah, me too. Most of us have. It is hard to stay focused on what we want when we are constantly confronted with stuff we don't have. Consumer spending is responsible for three quarters of the economy of the United States. Is it any surprise then that we are inundated with advertisements about what we don't have?

But, let's get back to your "I don't want" list. The benefit of such a list is that once you put something on the list, you don't need to waste any more time thinking about that 'non-want' again.

Think about what would happen if you put the following on your "I don't want" list?

"I don't want to be poor."

Unfortunately, saying *"I don't want to be poor"* gets translated into attracting *"I want to be poor."* Thus, if we leave our thought on the negative of this issue, we simply attract more 'being poor'.

To solve this problem, let me suggest two things you might consider doing. First, when you have important 'I don't wants' in your life related to things like love, money, happiness (*"I don't want to be poor, sick, or lonely"*), rephrase the statement as a positive and write it down on your "I want" list (*"I want to have plenty of money so I can feel good and free."*).

Finally, file your 'I Don't Want' list in the IDM file.

Be done with all that stuff that doesn't matter. Dispense with it with a shout of *"**Be gone, evil demon**!"* or some similar phrase. Whatever floats your boat.

Don't waste the valuable processing power of your subconscious with endless programs about what you don't want. Focus on what you do want and ignore the rest.

Now, some of you really smart people think that I tried to trick you into keeping two lists (the 'I don't want' list, and the 'I want' list.) Not so. If you follow the steps that I have given you, you end up with only one list, your 'I want' list. The 'I don't want' list is in the wastebasket.

In truth, you were right on target when you asked: *"If I spend all my time writing down what I don't want, how will I have time to focus on what I do want?"*

***

You won't have time to focus on what you do want if you spend all your time focused on what you don't want. So, don't do that. Simple, yes? Just the way I like it.

41
Helping Others Feel Good

Do you ever try to help other people feel good? Someone asked me the other day why I give to charitable causes? My answer was: *"To make myself feel good."*

The person's reaction to my response was not what I anticipated. He said:

"Well, that's a pretty selfish reason. Don't you want to make other people feel good, too? But, then, I guess you don't care much about how other people feel if the only person you ever think about is yourself."

Dang! I think I just got whammied! My teeth feel like they have been kicked and my butt doesn't feel much better.

This person didn't stick around long enough to give me a chance to explain myself. And, the truth is, we're probably both better off having him take his 'holier-than-thou' attitude somewhere else. Hopefully he can find people with whom he can vibrate more harmoniously.

Nevertheless, I still didn't appreciate being called an uncaring person. Had he stuck around long enough to hear my explanation, he might have learned something about himself that would have helped him be less judgmental of others (specifically...me!)

I didn't say: *"I don't care about how other people feel."* Actually, it's quite the opposite. I'm writing this book with the hope that some people will read it and improve the quality of their lives. However, I know something that the person who criticized me doesn't know.

I can't make another person feel good.

I can empathize with their feelings. I can offer support and comfort. I can listen to their troubles and offer my suggestions. I might be able to make them laugh or cry. But, the truth is, I can't make them feel better. The only person who can make us feel good is ourselves.

Too often, I hear people preach about how much they help others. They are quick to tell anyone who will listen about all the time and money and care they give. Now, don't misunderstand me; I appreciate what they do for others. But, what many people don't realize is that, <u>when we help others, we are really helping ourselves</u>. When we help others...<u>we feel good</u>.

When you see someone who isn't as fortunate as you, how do you feel? Does that person make you feel uncomfortable? Do you feel sick to your stomach when you see someone in poverty? Do you cringe at the thought of a child's empty belly? Do you feel an ache in your heart? Those are all reasonable feelings we have when we see someone who is less fortunate.

However, if we believe in the way attraction works, how is feeling bad going to help that other person? More importantly, how is feeling bad going to help us attract good feelings into our lives? It won't. Not now or ever. Feeling bad about the other person's situation is coming from a feeling of 'not having'.

"Look. That poor child doesn't have any shoes. And, she obviously hasn't had a good meal in weeks. I'll bet her parents are drug addicts. They probably don't know or even care where she is most of the time. Poor thing."

How do you feel when you read those words? Uplifted? Motivated? Happy with the world? I doubt it. You are probably feeling bummed-out, sad, perhaps even angry or depressed.

If that's the way you are feeling, what are you going to attract? More of the same. Is that really what you want in your life? More bad feeling? Of course not. Nobody does.

More importantly, if <u>you</u> feel bad, is that going to help the other person feel good? Hardly.

Let's take this same situation and see if we can attract some good feelings.

"Oh, look John. That child looks like she could use a little help. Let's take her over to the church and see if we can get her some clean clothes, a hot meal, and a little comfort. I'll bet she would like to have one of those dolls I put in the garage for the bazaar. I know we can't solve all her problems but, with a little help, maybe she can learn to feel better about herself."

Do you feel the difference? I imagine you feel better reading those words instead of the previous ones.

Are they good words to use to address the problem? Yes. These are words that are more focused on actions to bring about a positive solution. We want to focus on the vibrations the words create. Do these words help you vibrate in a more positive way toward this little girl's situation? If so, then they will make <u>you</u> feel good.

If you feel good, what will you attract? More good feelings. If this little girl has the chance to be around some 'good-feeling people' for even a little while, won't that help her create and attract good feelings of her own? I can only speak for myself, but I believe that thinking about helping a person in this way has the chance to make the situation better. Focusing on the negatives never will.

So, why do I donate to charities? I donate, first, to help <u>me</u> feel good. If I feel good, the person I want to help has a chance to feel better. If I feel bad, I just attract more misery into their life.

I realize that this concept of doing something for someone else so that <u>I</u> will feel better is counter-intuitive. Many of us were taught to think of others first. In fact, some of us were told that if we feel good while someone else is feeling bad, we should feel guilty about feeling good.

Well, I'm sorry, but I just don't agree. If I don't feel good, how can I possibly help someone else feel good. Besides, I can't <u>make</u> another person feel good. We can only make ourselves feel good.

I can't clear someone's personal vibrations for them. About all I <u>can</u> do is to emit good, clear vibrations of my own to attract good feelings for myself, and for those around me. So, until I find something that feels better, I'm going to continue to help others in a way that makes <u>me</u> feel good.

***

If you want to help someone feel good and help them improve the quality of their life, consider how <u>your</u> feelings will affect that other person's vibrations. The stronger and clearer you are about your feelings, the easier it will be for them to feel good about themselves.

42
A Simple Plan for Living

As I considered the concept of attraction and its relevance to my life, I found myself wanting one simple thought that would help me stay focused on what I want. The more I thought about it, the more I realized that the essence of attraction is about feeling good. With that in mind, I experimented with different phrases that made me feel good. One phrase stood out because it made me feel the best.

"I feel good about my life."

Yes, I know. This isn't poetic or life-changing wording. Shakespeare I'm not.

I also realize that this may sound too broad, not specific enough, not detailed enough to provide very good guidance. For some it may sound too Pollyannaish, unrealistic, and wishful. For others, it may not provide the tangible aspects they need to direct their daily lives. But, the more I thought about it, the more I realized that it provides me with the foundation upon which to build all of the aspects of my life. Let me tell you why.

Suppose someone gave you $10 million tomorrow. Would you feel good about that? Probably. Do you think you could feel good for the rest of your life if you had $10,000,000? Probably. But, let's think about this in another way.

How good would you feel if you had $10 million but you were stranded on a desert island? Even though you had the money and all the things it could buy, you had to live the rest of your life alone. How does that feel? I believe that the thought of having to live alone on a desert island for the rest of your life would not be a good feeling for most people. Just having the money would not make you feel good.

Let's take another example. Suppose you had all the money you needed and a wonderful person to share it with. But, suppose you also lost your sight, your hearing, your legs, or your arms? What if you were sick all the time? How would that feel?

Not so good, I'll bet.

When we take a look at how all the various aspects of our lives intertwine, I think we see how important it is to realize that what we do in one area can have a detrimental effect on another.

Let me be clear about my personal position on this matter. I want to feel good all the time, in all aspects of my life. Hey, I'm worth it, damn it! I deserve it. I have a right to feel good as much of the time as I can.

Where does it say that I have to feel bad a certain percentage of my life? Where is it written that I only get to be happy in certain parts of my life and not in others? Who says that we can't focus our intentions, wants and desires on feeling good all the time? I can't find any law that says we only get to be semi-happy.

But, if I seek to feel good in all aspects of my life, what does that mean as I move forward? It means that I need to let my feelings be my guide in everything I think, everything I seek, everything I do.

Can living life really be as simple as that? Could feeling good most of the time be the ultimate goal in life? I don't know, but I sure like the feel of it. But how will that thought and feeling actually work in real-time?

Let's assume that I have given serious consideration to the things I want to attract into my life. Suppose at a day-to-day level, my major wants are to be healthy, safe, happy, and prosperous, and to be around people who vibrate in harmony with me. How will this guide my decisions and actions?

"I like the thought of having $10,000,000. Actually, I even like the feeling I get when I think about having the money. But, am I willing to rob a bank or sell drugs to get that money? No, that doesn't feel good. Am I willing to work at something I like to do and take 20 years getting my $10,000,000? Yes, that feels just fine.

"Am I willing to work at a dangerous, high-paying job to make my money? No, that doesn't feel particularly good. Would I feel better if I worked at something where I will only earn $5,000,000 over the next twenty years, but where my likelihood of getting seriously injured or killed is significantly less? Yes, that definitely feels better.

"I could go to work at a higher-paying job overseas but that means I'll have to be gone from my family and friends for months at a time. How does that feel? Not very good. So, maybe I would feel better more of the time if I was not making as much money but had time to spend with family and friends.

"I really dislike my boss. How would I feel if I just up and quit? Well, part of me would feel great not having to face him/her every day and not having to put up with so much crap. However, the thought of not having any income does not make me feel good. Therefore, I

need to put my intentions toward finding a new job with someone I would like to work with. It feels good thinking about finding that new position over the next few months and keeping my income going in the meantime.

"I am fed-up with the relationship I have with my significant other. We argue and fight all the time. We don't seem to agree on anything anymore and we spend less and less time together. Maybe it's time to move on. I like the feeling of not fighting with someone for a while. But, if I leave him/her, I'll have to find someone else because I don't like living by myself.

"How do I feel about having to get out into the dating scene? Not so swell. And, what are the chances I will find someone who has many of the characteristics I really like about my current partner? Hard to know. Maybe I should talk with my partner and see if we can get some help refocusing our relationship. Maybe even get some counseling. Does that thought feel good? Well, it seems to feel better than just giving up on what we have.

"I'm really bored with my job. Maybe I could go back to school and get a degree in meteorology. I have always been fascinated by weather and I think that would be any area where I could get re-energized about what I do for a living. But, I can't just quit my present job. I don't want to graduate with $25,000 in student loans hanging over my head. That doesn't feel good. So, I think I will go to night school so I can continue earning enough to pay for my schooling."

Hopefully you are getting the idea here. Our lives are not made up of just one or two parts. Everything we do is related to all the other aspects of our lives. When we take action in one area, it is will have an impact on other areas. The trick is that we will attract what we want into our lives when we decide what our wants are and then focus our attention on fulfilling those wants. However, we cannot abandon the other areas of our life in the process.

So, when I think about the statement: *"I feel good about my life,"* it helps me remember to consider all the parts of my life as I make a decision. When I keep this phrase in mind as I go about my day, I find that it helps me keep my focus on the important things. It helps me to move past the little annoyances that have no bearing on the important areas of my life where I want to concentrate on feeling good.

***

Create your own phrase to help you maintain your focus on the important parts of your life. And, for the rest of the 'not-so-important-stuff', perhaps it's time to throw it in the IDM file.

43
Getting Your 'It' Together

In the *"Introduction"* I told you that my purpose in writing this book was to:

- Share information to help you focus your thoughts and actions to attract a better life;

- Offer ideas to help you reduce the amount of static in your life;

- Suggest ways to free yourself to live a life more in alignment with your natural self and your unique vibrations;

- Offer simple ideas to apply to the real-life situations you encounter everyday.

However, I also stated that I don't claim to have *"**The** Answer"*, or to know *"**The** Secret"* to creating a perfect life. I am not telling you *"**The** Way."* I only want to offer thoughts on how you can find *"**Your Way.**"*

I find the concept of attraction is a useful guide to having a better life. While I can't prove that there is a universal law of attraction that always determines what we attract into our lives, I have seen and experienced many effects that show me that this concept, or something like it, is at work in my life.

In many ways, *"like does attract like"*. Whatever we attract into our lives, we do so either by default, or by consciously deciding and focusing on what we want.

I often see that *"misery loves company."* But, I also see and experience the wonderful, positive vibrations that are generated when people are consciously working on getting their 'it' together.

Everything in the universe vibrates. Each of us has a frequency we are born with. This frequency is your soul, your inner being…your personal vibration. Regardless of what you call it, you have a vibrational frequency that defines who you are.

Too many of us allow our frequencies to be inundated with static. And, yes, I did say we <u>allow</u> it. Whether we exercise our right to choose or not, no one can create static in our systems unless we let them. Far too often we take on static because (1) we feel we don't have the right to have our own vibration; (2) we don't know how to make changes that would help us reduce or eliminate the static; or (3) we simply don't think about it.

Many of us are walled-in by the past, stuck in the muck of the present, and stressed-out worrying about the future. Unfortunately, none of these 'inactions' moves us closer to what we want.

While I can't prove that focusing my thoughts and actions and vibrations on attracting what I want will always work, I'm convinced that focusing on what I don't want has zero chance of working.

With that information in mind, let me offer these final thoughts about getting your 'it' together.

- You are born with a natural frequency that vibrates who you are.

- You have the right and responsibility to keep your frequency as clear as you want to it to be.

- No one can put static onto your system unless you let them.

- No amount of time or energy spent dwelling in the past or worrying about the future will ever get you closer to what you want.

- You are more likely to attract the life you want if you decide what is 'enough', and then focus your thoughts, actions and vibrations on moving toward what feels good.

I hope that something you read in this book will help you attract more of the good feelings you want in life. But, remember, <u>you are the only person who can get your 'it' together. No one else can do it for you.</u>

**

As for me, my Subconscious Processing Department just informed me that a donut hole has clogged up my black hole. So, I'd better get back to getting <u>my</u> 'it' together. Thanks for letting me share my thoughts.

GETTING YOUR 'IT' TOGETHER
Contact Information

If you would like to signup to receive a <u>FREE</u> subscription to the ***Getting Your 'It' Together*** newsletter, you can do so at <u>www.GettingYourItTogether.com</u>. This website also provides information on upcoming seminars, presentations, and other material of interest. You may also order additional books and audio book CD's through the site.

If you would like to have Hawkeye speak to your organization, you may contact him at the address below, or email him through his website. If you would like to comment on this book or share stories on how it has helped you, you can also write or send an email to:

Hawkeye Richardson
7925 N. Oracle Rd., PMB #176
Tucson, AZ 85704
Email/website: www.GettingYourItTogether.com

Hawkeye Richardson has been a business consultant and personal coach for over 30 years. Through personal coaching, he helps individuals to better balance their personal and work lives, and to focus on the things in life that are most important: family, friends, good health, an enjoyable and successful career, and a personal sense of well-being. As a business consultant,

Hawkeye also works with business owners and managers to help them find more effective, profitable and enjoyable ways to operate their companies.

Made in the USA